BRAND STRING THEORY
Make Your Brand Demand a Search Party
Written by Richard Every

© 2026 Richard Every. All rights reserved.

Brand String Theory™, Make Your Brand Demand A Search Party™, Commitment Isolation Test™, Brand Independence Test™, and all associated frameworks, methodologies, diagrams, and the complete system of 21 Brand Laws are the protected intellectual property of Richard Every and Richard Every Ltd.

The Internal Dimension (FORCE, FRAME, FUNCTION), External Dimension (CONCEPT, CONNECT, CONVERT), and Eternal Dimension (RECKONING, RECOGNIZE, RELEASE) organizational framework, along with all specific language, examples, and applications within this book, are copyright © 2026 Richard Every.

While Brand String Theory draws on universal principles of physics, brand behavior, and systematic thinking, the specific articulation, organization, and application of these principles as presented in this work represents original scholarship and proprietary methodology developed through 40 years of observing systems under pressure, from rugby fields to nightclub floors to boardrooms.

For rights inquiries, workshops, speaking, or licensing:
searchparty@brandstringtheory.com

Unauthorized reproduction, distribution, or commercial use of Brand String Theory methodology, frameworks, or terminology without written permission is strictly prohibited and subject to legal action. Educational references and brief quotations with proper attribution are welcomed under fair use.

ISBN (print): 979-8-218-75955-1 / ISBN (ebook): 979-8-218-76830-0

Cover Design: Richard Every & Anna Claude
Interior Design & Layout: Richard Every
Illustrations: Anna Claude
Editors: Anna Claude & Russel Wasserfall
Published by: Search Party Books
East Chatham, NY / Chicago, IL

Brand examples and case studies are used for educational analysis and commentary under fair use provisions. Some client references have been anonymized or used with permission.

MAKE YOUR BRAND
DEMAND A SEARCH PARTY

CONTENTS

INTRODUCTION   1

INTERNAL _____

FORCE Your Energy
1. Is your brand **Worth** the energy?   13
2. Are **Change**, challenge and inspiration available in your space?   23
3. If your brand **Disappeared**, would anyone know it was missing?   31

FRAME Your Structure
4. What **Belief** guides you in every creative or strategic decision?   41
5. What **Principle** guides what you do that others don't or won't do?   53
6. They remember one thing that your brand **Forged**. What would you want it to be?   61

FUNCTION Your Impact
7. Is your brand **Position** aligned?   71
8. When your brand **Works** what do people do?   79
9. Your customer journey delivers **Friction**. Good or bad?   87

INTERNAL CASE STUDIES:
WEWORK   94
APPLE   96
MANUFACTURER   98

EXTERNAL _____

CONCEPT Your Promise
10 The real **Hook.** Who are you talking to?   105
11 Your brand has only one **Sentence** to live by. What does it say? 113
12 Is your message relevant **Today**, or yesterday?   123

CONNECT Your Proof
13 **Benefits** separate your brand. Does your design back it up?   133
14 Attention. **Trust**. Where is it, and why is it there?   141
15 What brand sparks **Jealousy** (in a good way)?   149

CONVERT Your Payoff
16 There's **Commitment**. What happens next?   161
17 Why the **Excuse**, the hesitation?   169
18 When they say yes to their **Future**, what changes?   177

EXTERNAL CASE STUDY: DYSON   182
WORKING BRAND LAWS:
STANLEY   184
NETFLIX   186
DUOLINGO   187

ETERNAL _____

RECKONING Your Truth
19 Do you know the **Truth**, but haven't told anyone?   193

RECOGNIZE Your Vision
20 Your brand has **Vision**. What do you see?   203

RELEASE Your Independence
21 Your industry independence in seconds. Are you ready?   213

22 Your **Brand String Theory**. Your choice?   221

THE PROCESS   226
THE BRAND LAWS   227

INTRODUCTION

Imagine your brand vanished. Would anyone notice?

Your customers, your search party, are already out there. When they find you and connect, that is when you matter. Brand String Theory links every piece of your brand like evidence on a detective's board.

When everything is connected, there is a clear path to making sense of the whole.

Brand String Theory works like string theory in physics. Simple laws create infinite possibilities. Just as physicists theorize that everything in the universe connects through strings of energy, every part of your brand connects through strings of intent.

Most brands do not fail because they are bad. They fail because no one gives a damn. They disappear like buzzwords on a resume, fractional efforts delivering fractional results. They disappear because every decision needs to be micromanaged.

You know the feeling. You cannot explain what is wrong, you just know. You become the bottleneck holding everything up. It is not your fault. You were given inspiration without structure, positioning without foundation, and messaging without support.

The numbers prove it is getting worse. According to Forrester's 2024 US Customer Experience Index, **quality among brands sits at an all time low after declining for an unprecedented third year in a row, with only 3% of companies currently customer obsessed. This 3% outperforms everyone else, with faster revenue growth, higher profit growth, and stronger customer retention.**[1]

Most brands chase the order of the day, skipping the internal engine that makes them inevitable in the first place.

That is why Brand String Theory exists.
It is a structure. Not a style. Not a vibe. Not a trend.
It connects everything your brand builds, says, and does.

I learned the power of laws refereeing professional rugby. Most sports have rules that break under pressure. Rugby has laws that guide behavior under any condition.

| *Your brand needs laws, not rules.* |

Rules break under pressure. Laws eliminate complexity. Instead of managing endless brand guidelines, you gain clear direction that makes decisions easier. Instead of micro managing every detail, you trust your team to make the same choices you would.

That is freedom. That is confidence. That is what happens when your brand strings connect.

I did not always understand this. I have made every branding mistake there is. That journey taught me something crucial. Building a brand is not about looking cool. It is about being clear. Looking a little cool helps, but clarity is what lasts.

| *Under pressure, clarity is the first thing to leave the room.* |

When clarity goes, so does your brand.

Brand String Theory is for brands that want to matter. Not just to build awareness or maximize engagement, but to build something people care about.

This approach is not comfortable. If you want comfortable, you can keep doing what everyone else is doing. This is for brands that want to win.

Most brands start with the external. The logo. The website. The tagline. Brand String Theory starts with what drives you when no one is watching. The internal engine.

The theory.
The string.
The Brand String Theory.

Each chapter introduces a law, a field test, and a way to remove what does not matter.

Each of these laws is an operational value, not a component of an operating system. You don't install them. You live by them.

Together, they create clarity that performs under pressure.

When your brand's strings connect, nothing is accidental. Every decision makes sense. Every experience feels inevitable.

And if your brand disappeared tomorrow, people would notice.

Now let's begin.

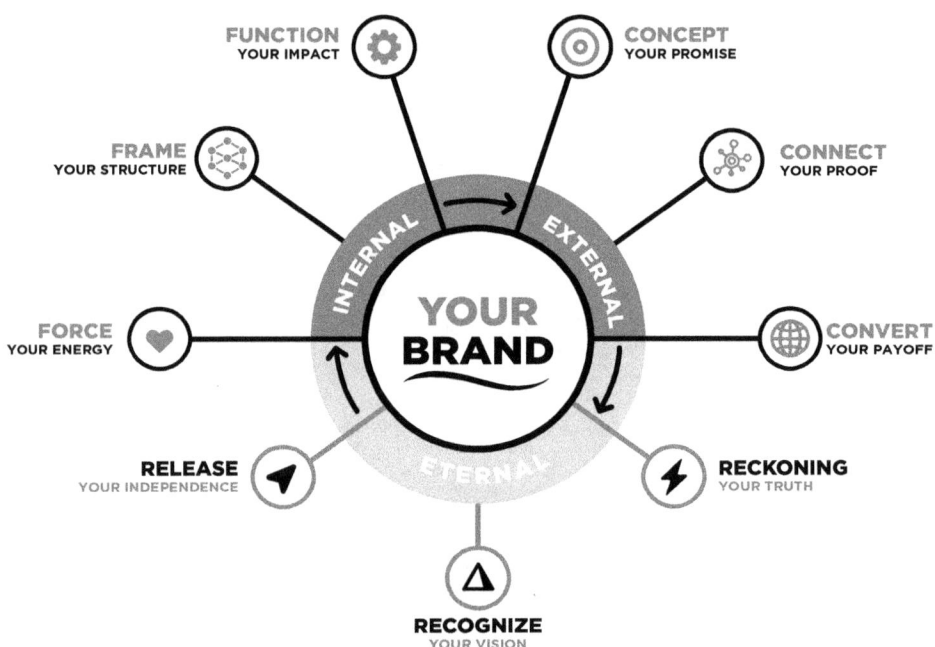

INTERNAL:
Where it all starts.

FORCE: YOUR ENERGY
What drives you when no one's watching.

FRAME: YOUR STRUCTURE
Your principle, your rhythm, your yes/no filter.

FUNCTION: YOUR IMPACT
Every touchpoint earns or loses trust.

EXTERNAL:
Where your brand meets the world.

CONCEPT: YOUR PROMISE
One sentence. One shot. Clarity wins.

CONNECT: YOUR PROOF
Design, tone, and behavior all pulling the same way.

CONVERT: YOUR PAYOFF
What happens next. Commitment is everything.

ETERNAL:
Where you declare your independence.

RECKONING: YOUR TRUTH
What do you want to be known for?

RECOGNIZE: YOUR VISION
What you see when everything connects.

RELEASE: YOUR INDEPENDENCE
The moment to deliver.

BRAND STRING THEORY

Where it all starts.
INTERNAL

FORCE
FRAME
FUNCTION

INTERNAL
FORCE

Brands aren't born with gravity.
You build it.
Your FORCE.
Guidance is internal.

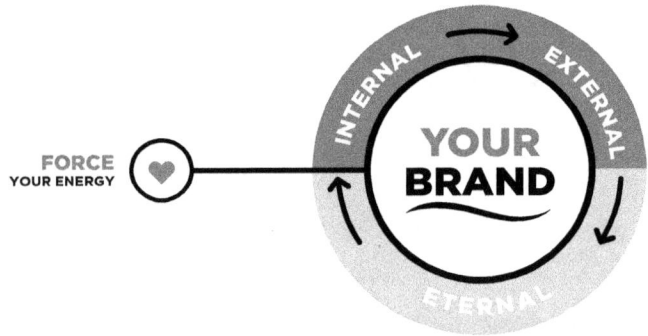

BRAND STRING THEORY

CHAPTER ONE
FORCE WORTH

IS YOUR BRAND WORTH THE ENERGY?

Most people start with the same formula: A mission statement that sounds like it was written by a committee, a paragraph about being "family-owned," and some vague adjectives like "trusted," "innovative," or "solution-focused" sprinkled across their homepage like emotional MSG.

It's safari branding.

Picture this: You're on safari in an open vehicle. A lion can walk past you, look you in the eye, and not see you. Not see that there's free lunch on top of a metal object. They see it all as one blob. That's safari branding. A bunch of brands out of their comfort zone pretending to be comfortable, all blending into one indistinguishable mass. Invisible targets.

I am not the biggest fan of safari branding. Sure, it's safe, neutral, and comfortable, but is that what you want for your brand? For your life? Not to offend, but to blend?

On the other side of the spectrum, you've got the Mirror Guy brands. We all know that guy. They're screaming how "innovative" or "revolutionary" they are, checking themselves out in every possible reflection, making every conversation about themselves. These brands demand to be admired and force-feed "I'm special" to the world. Their copy reads like it was written while gazing into a mirror, without any self-reflection. Every line engineered to shout "Pick me!"

My son Sam once confronted me about an outrageous claim: "Are you lying for attention?"

That's exactly what Mirror Guy brands do.

They lie for attention.
Their audience? Lost somewhere around paragraph one.

| Most brands are Mirror Guy or on safari. |

But what if you started from who you really are, from your foundation? In Brand String Theory, your foundation is your FORCE. It's the belief behind the brand, the reason you're willing to do this over and over again even when it's hard, unrewarding, or worse, ignored. It's the edge that says you don't exist to be liked; you exist because something wasn't good enough until you showed up.

REALITY CHECK: Sports Video Software Company
They had great technology but couldn't explain why match officials needed it. Their messaging focused on the problem they were solving. It concentrated on the great idea they had to develop officials' skills.

We discovered their FORCE. Officials want to be respected, not criticized. Their new positioning became "Become the referee everyone wants on their game." Now officials see the software as career advancement, not just technology. Result: It became the standard for referee development across North America.

But first, consider this: You're always building relationships or breaking them down. There's no middle ground.

In our hearts, we all know that it's true. When you're talking to someone, you can build the relationship or not. And when you need to function under pressure, being prepared is everything.

I had so many moments as a referee where it was critical to have empathy. Understanding the pressure players feel and responding with authority and humanity is what kept control of the game.

The good news is, you don't need to build your foundation by developing an endless slide deck. No need for vision boards, or endless workshops.

You can find it in the reason, or the frustration, that got you started.
In the pattern you see that no one else is fixing.
It's what you believe down to your core.

Even if it doesn't initially test well in a focus group, it will develop the more you understand who you are.

So what fuels you beyond the work itself?
It's not a tagline. It's who you are under pressure.
Many never find it because they're too busy trying to sound right, going on safari, or being Mirror Guy brands, instead of being honest.

But without your core, your FORCE, your brand is a shell. A mood-stricken mood board with no purpose.

Look at your last three big decisions. Did you make them based on what you believe, what seemed safe, or what your competitors were doing?

Here's what it looks like out there when you get it right.

Real Estate
Sellers deserve equity protection. They should keep more of what they've built. 1% commission isn't a discount. It's just fair.

Branding Agency
We exist to destroy the notion that safe is smart.
Safe blends in, and safe is risky.

Sustainable Packaging
We're here to end throwaway culture, one package at a time.
We design for what happens after the unboxing.

Healthcare Billing
We want hidden fees in healthcare eliminated. Everyone should know what it costs to get well.

Notice how specific these are? "We believe sellers should keep more." Not "We're committed to excellence."
The data backs this up.

Research from SAP Emarsys in 2024 shows that **true loyalty driven by emotional connections has grown by 26% since 2021, reaching 34% in 2024, while customers with emotional connection to brands have a 306% higher lifetime value.**[2]

Brands with a real FORCE behind them are more likely to be shared, remembered, and trusted.

Look at the giants who get this:
LEGO is not just about play; it's about inspiring builders of tomorrow.

Patagonia isn't about clothes; it's about protecting what's left.
Tony's Chocolonely isn't just tasty; it's about ending child labor in chocolate.
Walmart shifted from being seen as purely transactional to pursuing large-scale sustainability. They're not just about everyday low prices anymore; it's about everyday impact, making sustainability, opportunity, and belonging accessible to everyone.

These aren't slogans.
Each is a FORCE to be reckoned with.
Not every FORCE changes the world. But..
A strong FORCE will change someone's world.

| *Every strong FORCE changes someone's world.* |

And drives everything.

If your whole team had to explain what you stand for in one breath, would they all say the same thing?

Or would it sound like amateur improv night?

That's how you test it.
If you can't say it clearly, no one can follow it.

In Brand String Theory, it's like this:
Every second is an impression. And if you don't show up as a FORCE, focused, and building relationships, you easily become forgettable.

Your FORCE is invisible, but like gravity, it affects every

decision that enters its field. Get this right, and every other choice falls into natural orbit around it. It drives how you design, how you write, and how you work.

You don't know the real strength of your brand until the lights go out. That's when you discover if your strings strengthen under pressure.

You're adding the first piece of evidence to the board. Your FORCE is the anchor point, the element that forms the foundation to everything else. Everything connects to this.

So what makes your brand Worth the energy?

Write it. Say it.
If it takes a paragraph, keep going.
Write it again. Say it again.
Repeat, until you get it to where it's all Worth the effort.

Use it like your brand (your life) depends on it.

Because it does.

FORCE WORTH BRAND LAW

Your **Worth** in one sentence drives everything.

YOUR FORCE WORTH FIELD TEST

1. **What was the reason or frustration that got you started?**
   Pinpoint the problem that made you take action.

2. **If your whole team had to explain what you stand for in one sentence, would they all say the same thing?**
   Ask three people. If answers are clear and consistent, you're focused.

3. **Did your last three big decisions reflect your core belief, or just what was safe?**
   Review any major choice and make sure it's driven by what you stand for.

LESS IS MORE

Instead of juggling multiple "core values," you now have one FORCE that guides every decision.
You just eliminated 80% of your brand confusion.

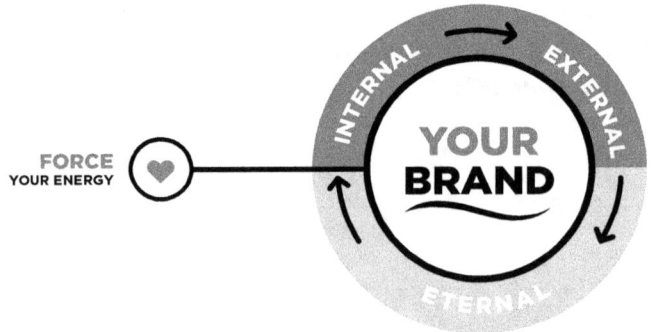

BRAND STRING THEORY

CHAPTER TWO
FORCE CHANGE

ARE CHANGE, CHALLENGE, AND INSPIRATION AVAILABLE IN YOUR SPACE?

Every brand that matters fights.

Pushing against what's broken, outdated, or just plain stupid in their industry. They're saying "It doesn't have to be this way" while everyone else shrugs and accepts the status quo.

If you're not trying to Change something, you're adding to the pile. The pile is overpopulated. It's a tough place to compete. However...

| **The status quo is not your enemy, it's your guide.** |

Running a nightclub taught me that everyone hears the same music differently. The soundtrack to your life is personal. When you hear something that matters to you, it becomes unforgettable.

And the moment you Change one thing, everything shifts. We divided music into genres and shifted from one genre into another every two songs without fail, and the result was a massive and more-engaged audience. Every person felt like the club was a soundtrack for their life. Revolutionary? No. But it started a movement that people still talk about today.

But this is very important. You don't need to revolutionize your entire industry. You just need to fix the one thing that's always annoyed you about how business gets done.

It applies to every industry. Brands accept "that's just how it's done," as gospel. That phrase is where opportunities hide.

The IBM Institute of Business Development reports that **44%**

of consumers today are purpose-driven, choosing products and brands that align with their values, marking them as the largest consumer segment, while 30% of consumers are influenced by ethical considerations in their brand loyalty.[4] Translation: Customers don't just want products; they want brands that stand for something. Purpose beats profit margins.

What's your stand?
Take a stand. Challenge the way things are.

REALITY CHECK:
Tesla didn't just build electric cars. They declared war on the lie that "sustainable" meant "boring." Before Tesla, electric vehicles were golf carts. After Tesla, they were status symbols with zero emissions and zero compromises. They didn't join the industry, they changed the rules everyone was playing by.

That's what your FORCE does. It fights the industry's biggest lie.

Other common examples are:
TOMS challenged the concept that commerce and charity had to be separate.
Allbirds took on the sneaker industry's obsession with synthetic materials.
Oatly picked a fight with dairy and wasn't polite about it.

There are three ways your FORCE creates Change.

Cleaning: Brands that exist because something in their industry actively hurts people. Healthcare companies fighting hidden fees. Financial services fighting predatory lending. Software companies fighting unnecessarily complex interfaces. (Like TURQUOISE HEALTH, CHIME, and STRIPE.)

Disrupting: Brands that want people to act differently. An app that made daily mindfulness a trend. Environmental companies promoting sustainable choices. Education brands encouraging lifelong learning. (HEADSPACE, THREDUP, and MASTERCLASS are examples.)

Pioneering: Brands that are not fixing what's broken, they're showing what's possible. Luxury brands redefining quality. Service companies repositioning customer experience. Tech companies driving what's user-friendly. (Look at BANG & OLUFSEN, TRADER JOE'S, and ZOOM.)

What's your industry's biggest lie? Every industry has one: That foundational assumption everyone accepts but nobody questions.

"Healthy food can't taste good."
"Professional services have to be boring."
"Quality costs more."
"Customer service is a cost center."
"Financial advice is only for the wealthy."

Find your industry's biggest lie and make it your mission to prove it wrong.

As a referee, for me, the biggest lie was that authority meant being unapproachable. Everyone expects referees to be intimidating and distant to be fair. But that's not the truth.

Treating players with dignity and respect while maintaining authority gives the referee more control over the game, and creates a better environment.

The same applies in business. Find what everyone accepts as truth and ask: "What if it's not?" Your competitors believe the same lies you used to believe. When you stop believing them, you get a head start.

Here's how you know if your Change actually matters:
Does it make people say: "Finally, someone gets it"?
Does it solve a problem people didn't even realize they had?
Does it make competitors scramble to catch up?
Does it attract talent wanting to be part of something meaningful?

If your answer to any of these is yes, you're onto something.

If your answer to all of them is no, you need to fix something.

Here's a deeper view of what it looks like.

Warby Parker looked at eyewear and saw an industry controlled by Luxottica charging hundreds of dollars for frames that cost little to make. So they asked a simple question: "What if we sold directly and cut out the middleman?"

Different pricing. Different distribution. Different approach to trying before buying. Their goal was not to make slightly cheaper glasses. They changed what glasses could cost. The Japanese minimalist retailer **MUJI** got sick of choice overload. While retailers shoved thousands of products at customers, MUJI said no. No logos, no brands, no more. Just things that work. Their "no-brand" obsession proved that less wins. Now they have 1,000+ stores globally because they competed on clarity, not selection.

And here's a great example of something that annoyed somebody.

BagUps make biodegradable trash bags. Great. But what really annoys us? Every time we take the trash out, we have to replace the bag. The BagUps box fits tightly into the bottom of your trash can, so you now have a conveyor belt of trash bags. And they're biodegradable! And veteran-owned.

Now what?
Don't think innovation, think specifically: What you are trying to Change? What assumption in your industry is wrong?

What would happen if you succeeded? Answer that in one sentence, and you have a fight worth fighting.

Because if you're not changing anything, it's tougher to let someone know you're here. The world needs companies that do things better.

Think about the dumbest thing everyone in your industry accepts as normal.

Fix that, and you could be onto something.

FORCE CHANGE BRAND LAW

Change the industry norm that competitors accept.

YOUR FORCE CHANGE FIELD TEST

1. **What's the industry norm everyone accepts?**
   Look for accepted practices that hurt customers or hold back progress.

2. **What would competitors never do?**
   Find opportunities where your approach lets you act but their approach stops them.

3. **If you succeeded, what would be different for your customers or industry?**
   Define the specific Change you're trying to create, not just what you're selling.

LESS IS MORE

You stopped competing with everyone and started building something only you can deliver. Your strategy just simplified to clear distinction.

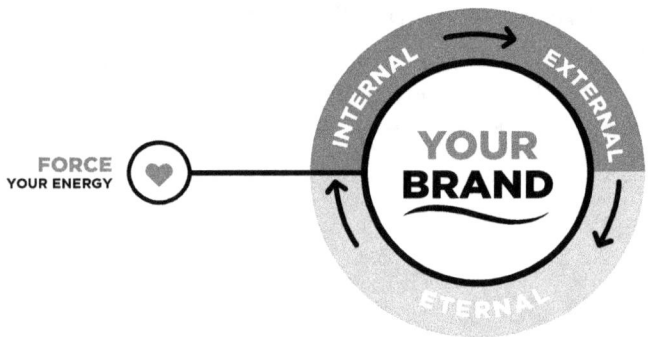

BRAND STRING THEORY

CHAPTER THREE
FORCE DISAPPEARED

IF YOUR BRAND DISAPPEARED, WOULD ANYONE KNOW IT WAS MISSING?

Be honest: If your brand vanished, what hole would it leave?

Not hypothetically. Not from your point of view; from your customers'. Check their emails to you. Do they thank you for doing your job, or for caring about something bigger?

What would your customers miss?
What emotional void would open up?
What practical thing would stop working in their life?

Because if your answer is "good service" or "great product", you're every other brand.

This isn't just about being liked. It's about being needed, then being liked. It's about becoming the thing they trust, depend on, and talk about when you're not in the room.

Connected customers are worth more.

Yet traditional **brand loyalty declined from 77% in 2022 to just 69% in 2024, while 61% of consumers switched** some or all of their business from one brand to another in the last year according to Capital One Shopping.[3]

The brands winning are those building real emotional connections. The value is less price-sensitive.

And you can't manufacture emotional connection. It happens when customers see you actually care about the thing you say you care about.

| *They will advocate for you like their reputation depends on it.* |

REALITY CHECK: Indoor Air Quality Company
They were lost in advanced air cleaning systems' technical complexity when trying to sell air quality systems to schools. Drowning in jargon about "advanced UVC-LED air purification technology for HVAC systems" that meant nothing to decision-makers. We discovered what parents would really miss: Confidence that their kids are safe at school. The repositioning to "100% Science, 100% Safer" shifted their focus from facilities' managers to the administration, teachers, and parent advocates. The cold outreach of "PARENTS AGREE: 100%. Their children get sick at school." proved endlessly successful with an astronomical click-through rate of over 50% and conversion of 30%.

So what happens when you're gone?

Because if nobody misses your brand, you didn't build a brand; you filled a space in the market. Market spaces get replaced. Brands get defended.

Brands stay with people.

Useful isn't enough.
Your brand might solve a real problem.
That's step one. But practical utility doesn't build loyalty, it just earns a spot in the rotation.

You're not trying to be an option. You're trying to be the answer.

Here's the line you have to cross:
From function... to feeling.
From "it works" to "I trust it."
From "nice to have" to "how did we live without it?"
Emotional Connection = Brand Strength.

Convenience that feels like care. Innovation that feels like freedom. Support that feels like understanding. That's what you're really offering. Because "we deliver fast" isn't good enough.

Many can deliver. Few can be trusted.

Look at **Zappos**. Powered by Service.
They didn't invent online shopping. They didn't even invent free returns. They just made customer service feel like a relationship.
Their customers didn't just buy, they bragged. They told stories.
Because it felt like someone actually gave a damn.

And when it feels like someone cares that much, you don't want to let go.

What About **Canva**? Bring your ideas to life in minutes.
They didn't invent design. They just removed the gatekeepers. They said, "You want to make something beautiful? You should be able to."

That's emotional empowerment. That's why their users don't just use Canva, they identify with it. Whether it delivers professional work depends on the user.

| *You can't fake that you care. You have to earn it.* |

And then there's **Kicking Horse Coffee!** Wake up. Kick ass. They didn't start in Brooklyn. They started in a garage in the Canadian Rockies, "pretty much near the middle of nowhere." Kicking Horse didn't just sell coffee, they dared you to Kick Ass.

It's organic, fair-trade Arabica, roasted right in the Rockies, not to sound fancy, but to guarantee that flavor and ethics actually link. They went all the way: bold, unapologetic, and unforgettable. It wasn't just coffee, it was an identity. And the coffee kicks.

Earth Breeze makes sustainable cleaning products, but with their Hope Cloth, they're missing their best story. The dishcloth never stinks. That musty, moldy smell that ruins kitchen towels? Gone. They solved the one problem every kitchen hates most but instead of hammering it, they wallpaper it with sustainability stats. That's not strategy. That's hiding the very thing people would actually miss if it disappeared.

So what's missing without you?

If you Disappeared, what gap would open up?
A community that felt real?
A problem no one else was solving?
A quality that others won't touch?
A voice that actually feels human?
A cloth that never stinks?

And more importantly, would anyone fight to keep you? Would anyone email the CEO, the founder, someone? Would they take to social media? Send out a search party? Try to rebuild it?

That's the goal.

Think of it this way: Demanding a search party is not about vanishing, it's about being here and now. It's where practical meets personal. This isn't about writing a sob story.

| *It's about being part of someone's story.* |

The moments that matter. The routines that stay. The help they didn't expect but now rely on.

That's the bar.

Relevance Pressure Test
Let's ask the CEO and Founder of **SPOT**, the 1% commission real estate firm in Chicago.

What unique solutions or experiences do you offer that others don't?
"We are the new standard the real estate industry has been avoiding. Full-service professional representation at 1% commission. Not a discount. Not a compromise. The standard that 2.5-3% never deserved to be."

How do customers emotionally connect with your brand?
"Vindicated. 91% of people say they'll use the same realtor again. Only 17% do. Not because the agent failed them.

Because the system did. SPOT is the first company that makes the whole transaction feel honest. The sale. The service. The check at closing."

What gap would exist in the market without your presence?
"The standard reverts to traditional agents charging premium prices for regular services while pretending they control buyers who actually find houses online, or sellers whose homes are listed online. Flat fee companies would continue to list properties without support. We are not the missing middle. We are the new standard."

If SPOT Disappeared, would people be left in a bad place?
Homeowners lose tens of thousands of dollars at the most important transaction of their lives, and no one has to admit the math was always broken. The extraction continues. The standard never gets set.

When you tackle these questions, don't guess.

Be direct. Be specific. Be honest.

If your customers have never said it out loud, your brand's job is to give them the words through everything you are, everything you do, and everything you represent.

This is your Monday morning alarm without a snooze button. No one misses generic. No one fights for safari brands. No one sheds a tear over yet another Mirror Guy's "innovative" or "self-ranked" #1 product that looks like all the others.

You want to know if your brand matters?
Imagine taking it away for a day, a week, a month.
And if you feel nobody will notice, then start again.

Check:
Do they need you, or do they need what you do?
Do they buy from you, or do they buy into you?
Are you a vendor, or are you their choice?
What happens when a competitor offers the same thing for less?
What happens when someone else does it faster?
What happens when the market shifts?

People don't miss logos.
They miss how you make them feel.

How you make their life easier, clearer, better, sharper.

How you make them brag about having you in their life.

Your brand should always deserve a search party.

That's what you build!

FORCE DISAPPEARED BRAND LAW

Build a brand they'd miss forever if it **Disappeared**.

YOUR FORCE DISAPPEARED FIELD TEST

1. **If you vanished tomorrow, what would your customers miss?**
   Do customers thank you for doing your job or for caring about something bigger?

2. **Do they need you, or do they need what you do?**
   If a competitor offered the same service for less, would your customers switch or fight to keep you?

3. **What's the quick benefit a fan would actually tell a friend?**
   It should be clear in one sentence. A short one.

LESS IS MORE

You stopped trying to be everything to everyone and started being essential to someone.
Your marketing just became 5X more focused.

BRAND STRING THEORY

INTERNAL FRAME

Consistency is not luck.
You build it.
Your FRAME.
To strengthen under pressure.

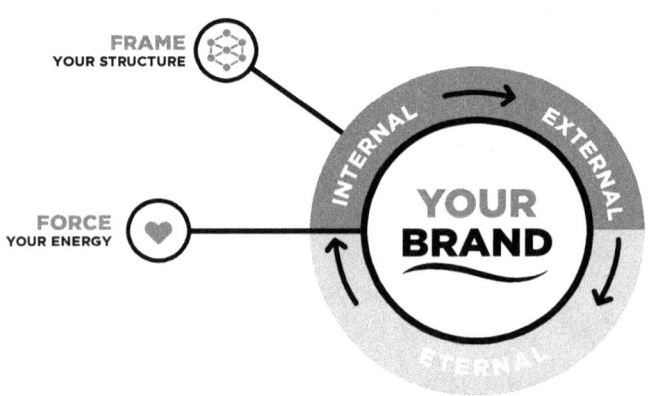

BRAND STRING THEORY

CHAPTER FOUR
FRAME BELIEF

WHAT BELIEF GUIDES YOU IN EVERY CREATIVE OR STRATEGIC DECISION?

Your brand FORCE gives you purpose. Your FRAME gives you process.

It's the difference between knowing what you stand for and knowing how to act on it. Every day. In every decision. Under every kind of pressure. It stands on the shoulders of your FORCE.

Often brands wing it. They make choices based on what feels right in the moment, what the competitor down the street is doing, or whatever the intern with the design degree suggests. Then they wonder why their brand feels scattered.

A psychiatrist once told me: Being mean, aggressive, and judgmental is easy. It's quitting on choice altogether. Being patient, calm, and supportive? That's hard. That's a series of deliberate decisions under pressure.

Your FRAME is your decision-making DNA. It's what you always say yes to, what you always say no to, and why. It's the filter that makes every business and creative choice feel inevitable instead of arbitrary.

My wife Anna, an architect, designs from the inside out. The internal intent, the flow, and the purpose of each space determine everything you see on the outside. It's about integrity.

Brands work the same way. Your internal FRAME, your Belief about how you do business, should drive every external decision. When the internal structure is well thought out and solid, the external expression feels effortless.

| *Your FRAME Belief is your yes/no machine.* |

Think about it like this... Many successful brands don't question whether something matters. They simply do it, and they do it consistently. These aren't discussions: They're givens.

Because when you know what you believe, deciding becomes easier.

Here's what I've learned from every creative disaster I've survived: When you don't have a clear Belief driving your choices, you get design-by-committee. And that's how you end up looking like you're on safari.

You know the moment when the logo gets passed around? One wants it bolder. Another wants it softer. Your mom wants it blue because she likes blue. Their opinions make sense to them, but none of them see your brand the way you do. They don't see how you've built your brand around your FRAME.

We've all been in conference rooms where someone says, "Maybe we should ideate some disruptive innovations to maximize stakeholder engagement," and everyone nods because nobody knows what the brand really stands for. I've watched brands chase trends instead of staying true to their framework, then wonder why their customers are never quite sure what they're doing.

Today it's a custom project; tomorrow, it's a worthless warranty.

"Ideate" is not a real word.

Your framework answers the question every creative and strategic choice poses:

"Does this fit who we are?"
Not "Does this look cool?"
Not "Will this go viral?"
But "Is this us?" What Belief guides every choice?

IBM's 2022 study found that **62% of consumers are willing to change their purchasing habits to reduce environmental impact.**[5] But here's the thing. People can smell fake from a mile away. Consistent values baked into actual decisions create trust. Inconsistent values that only show up in marketing create skepticism.

Look at how Belief drives decisions:

Apple: Intuitive design isn't negotiable.
Every interface, every button, every swipe follows the same belief: Technology should feel human. They don't ask "Can we make this more complex?" They ask "Can we make this simpler?" Same framework, different applications.

Figma: The default is collaboration.
They didn't take a solo design tool and bolt on sharing. Collaboration is the foundation. Every decision runs through one belief: design shouldn't happen in isolation. No emailing files. No version chaos. One shared source of truth, built for multiplayer work.

Hiut Denim: Craft over everything.
They only make jeans. They could expand into jackets, shirts, and accessories, but their framework says craft matters more than growth. They're not trying to be the biggest denim company. They're working to be the best at what they do.

Notice how specific these are? Not "We believe in excellence" or "We're customer-focused." Generic garbage that every brand claims.

Your framework should be specific enough that it eliminates options.

Your Belief works like a molecular bond. It determines what sticks to your brand and what gets repelled. Strong bonds create stable structures. Weak bonds fall apart under pressure.

When you know what you always say yes to, you automatically know what to say no to.

Here's how to find yours:
Look at your last three major decisions. What guided them? What did you refuse to compromise on? What felt non-negotiable?

If you can't find a pattern, you don't have a FRAME yet. You have preferences. Preferences change with moods. Your FRAME guides consistency.

Here's the difference in action:
A design company has a preference for "clean design." When a client wants more features on the homepage, they

debate aesthetics and eventually compromise with a cluttered interface.

But a software company with a framework that says "Confused users don't convert" doesn't debate. They automatically say no to anything that creates confusion, regardless of client pressure or competitor tactics. The decision is already made.

Preferences are opinions.
Your FRAME is built on laws. Like gravity, they don't waver.

Laws are forged through consequence. A belief that has never cost you anything is still a preference.

When you know your laws, decisions become automatic.

Let's say you're a financial advisory firm. Your FRAME might be: "Clarity protects wealth."
Now every decision filters through this Belief:

Complex products? Rejected (they obscure clarity).
Dense legal jargon? Simplified (it confuses clients).
Hidden fees? Eliminated (they destroy trust through opacity).
Privacy protocols? Non-negotiable (protect wealth through privacy).

One belief. Multiple applications. Deliberate decisions.

FRAME Belief Test
It's working when: Team members make decisions that feel like you made them. Customers trust how you'll respond to industry changes.

Competitors can't copy your approach because they don't share your Belief.

You can say no to profitable opportunities that don't fit, and often they don't benefit you long-term anyway. If you're still debating basic brand decisions, your FRAME isn't clear enough.

Your Belief should eliminate most creative discussions. Not because you're limiting creativity, but because you're focusing it. When everyone knows what the brand always does and never does, you don't start from: "What do we do?" You start with: "How do we do this better?"

That's when your brand stops feeling random and starts feeling inevitable.

FRAME BELIEF BRAND LAW

Your **Belief** is your yes/no machine.

YOUR FRAME BELIEF FIELD TEST

1. **What do you always say yes to, even when it's expensive?**
   Identify what you prioritize over profit; this reveals your true framework.

2. **What do you always say no to, even when might prove profitable?**
   Find what is not negotiable, the things you won't compromise on for money.

3. **Do team members make decisions that feel like you made them?**
   Test if your Belief is clear enough to guide others without your input.

LESS IS MORE

Your team now makes decisions like you would, even when you're not there. You eliminated creative debates and brand confusion. Leadership just got easier.

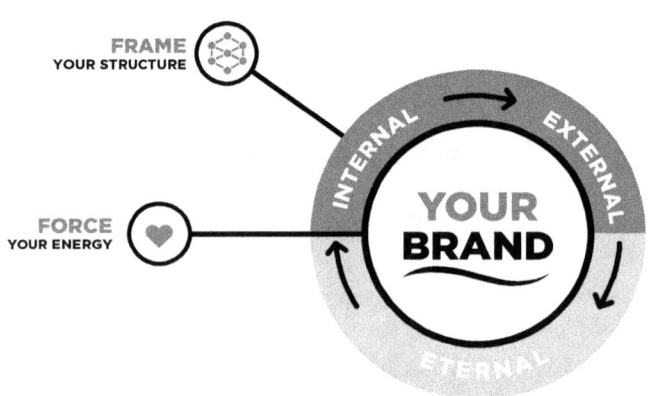

BRAND STRING THEORY

CHAPTER FIVE
FRAME PRINCIPLE

WHAT PRINCIPLE GUIDES WHAT YOU DO THAT OTHERS DON'T OR WON'T DO?

Most brands think differentiation means being louder. Differentiation means being definitively you. It's doing something your competitors don't (or won't) do. Not because they can't figure it out, but because it doesn't fit who they are.

Your dominance isn't about outshouting everyone else. It's about doing the thing that makes people say, "Of course they did that."

This is where your FRAME becomes visible. Where your Belief turns into behaviors. Where what you DO and DON'T DO becomes your signature.

| *If your competitors can copy you, you're not different.* |

My sports video software company nearly failed before I understood this. We'd build features our competitors didn't have, and vice versa. Everyone was scrambling to match. We were like cats chasing laser dots.

Features are easy to copy. Behaviors based on a Principle? Impossible. We finally realized competitors couldn't fake our conviction that professional development was broken, that people needed real structure, not just another training platform. That's when we started building what we believed.

REALITY CHECK: Industrial Manufacturer
This client makes serious industrial equipment. The kind with extensive supply chains, quality control processes, and testing protocols that would make NASA jealous. In fact, they built custom components for aerospace labs.

Everything about their business screamed "This takes time."

They had something competitors couldn't match: Precision-engineered systems shipped in five business days. Not weeks. Days.

Their competitors took 4–12 weeks minimum for the same work. Why the difference? While everyone else waited for purchase orders to start manufacturing, they pre-assembled the most common configurations and kept them in stock. They restructured their entire warehouse strategy around getting customers what they needed when they needed it.

Competitors could have done the same thing, but their frameworks prioritized lean inventory over customer speed. Different Belief, different results.

What do customers remember? "They deliver as promised."

Here's what Qualtrics XM Institute found: **89% of companies with "significantly above average" customer experiences perform better financially than their competitors.**[6] But here's what they didn't mention: It's not the experience itself that matters, it's the FRAME behind it.

So what's your Principle?

Look at brands that get this:

Costco: "We trust you."
Their return policy is insane. You can return almost everything (even a membership), and get your money back. Their

competitors think this is financially reckless. Costco's framework says trust creates loyalty, and loyalty beats transaction-by-transaction profit. Competitors won't do this because they don't trust their customers.

Spotify: "Music is personal."
They don't just give you access to songs. They learn what you like and create playlists you didn't know you needed. Discover Weekly. Release Radar. Wrapped. Their competitors see music as inventory.

Monzo: "Banking should be transparent."
Real-time notifications for every transaction. No hidden fees. Spending insights that actually help. Traditional banks won't do this because their business model relies on opacity. 12 million customers in 10 years with over 90% customer satisfaction.

Notice none of these are about having more features or better technology. They're about applying a different Belief to the same challenges everyone faces. They are Principles.

Your "Won't Factor"
Your edge isn't just something you do that competitors don't. It's something you do that they won't.
Because doing it would require them to believe something they don't.

But here's what happens when you abandon your "Won't Factor":
Tesla's Belief was: Electric should outperform gas.
Their Principle: Performance without compromise.

For over a decade, Tesla delivered. Every model existed to prove that electric is premium. Faster off the line, longer range, smarter engineering.

Along came the Cybertruck. This was the moment Tesla stopped following its own FRAME. The obsession with stainless steel and a futuristic silhouette replaced performance. It exposed real cracks: quality-control issues, multiple recalls, inconsistent panels, and basic usability concerns. They broke their Belief and their Principle.

Finding Your "Won't Factor"
Ask yourself:
What do you do that feels obvious to you but seems crazy to others?
What Principle guides your decisions that competitors ignore?
What would you refuse to change even if it cost you money?

That industrial manufacturer won't wait for purchase orders to start production. They pre-assemble configurations because delivery speed beats lean inventory.

As a referee, I won't be unapproachable to seem fair. Dignity and respect with authority works better than intimidation, even when everyone expects the opposite.

FRAME Principle Test

Your differentiator is working when:
- Customers choose you specifically because of your Principle.
- Competitors copy your tactics but can't copy your consistency.

- Your team naturally starts doing this without being trained.
- You'd rather lose business than compromise on it.

Most brands have preferences.
A great brand has a Principle.
Preferences break under pressure.
Principles guide under pressure.
Principle as a Law. Unshakable, predictable, unstoppable.
Here's the truth.

Your competitors are watching. They see what works for you. If it's just a feature or a service offering, they'll copy it. But if it's rooted in a FRAME they don't share, they'll struggle to replicate it.

Because FRAME-driven differentiation isn't about what you do; it's about why you do it. And that's much harder to fake. When your edge comes from your Principle, it becomes sustainable. When it comes from your features, it's temporary. What's something you do that your competitors don't, or won't? If you can't answer that clearly, you're competing on price.

And that's a race to the bottom.

Build something that comes from who you are, not just what you offer.

FRAME PRINCIPLE BRAND LAW
Your **Principle** makes every deliverable decision obvious.

YOUR FRAME PRINCIPLE FIELD TEST
1. **What do you offer, that your competitors simply cannot?** Identify a Principle that sets you apart. 2. **What do you do that feels obvious to you but crazy to others?** Your "obvious" choice reveals a Principle competitors don't share. 3. **How does your Principle eliminate most options and help you make more obvious decisions?** If it doesn't eliminate unnecessary choices, it's not strong enough to run your brand.

LESS IS MORE
You stopped chasing features and started owning a Principle. You eliminated the fear of being copied because your advantage now comes from your Laws, not your latest release.

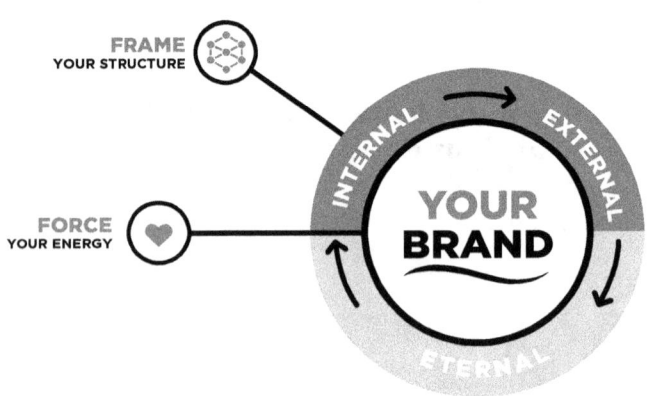

BRAND STRING THEORY

CHAPTER SIX
FRAME FORGED

THEY REMEMBER ONE THING THAT YOUR BRAND FORGED. WHAT WOULD YOU WANT IT TO BE?

If someone experienced your brand and could only remember one thing about it, what would you want that to be?

Your logo, your tagline, how many awards you've won or how many years you've been in business? None of that matters if it's forgotten by Thursday.

What moment or feeling is going to stick?
Because if nobody remembers you, you're part-time.

Countless brands optimize for everything, which means they're memorable for nothing. They want to be known for quality AND innovation AND customer service AND sustainability AND being family-owned since 1843.

By the time they're done listing their virtues, the customer's out the door.

| *You can't be memorable for everything.* |

In nightclubs nobody remembers the decor, the drink list, or the odd song. The set is the thing. The story. That makes them feel like songs were chosen specifically for them. That's what Forged the connection.

And once it's Forged, it's the one thing that lasts.

Memory is a thief.
Brands don't realize: Every additional thing you try to be remembered for steals memory from everything else.

| **Memory isn't additive. It's competitive.** |

When you try to own five things, you own nothing. When you own one thing completely, it owns everything else.

But here's what others won't tell you... You can't just pick your one thing from a menu. You can't brainstorm your way to memorable. You have to Forge it.

| *Your one thing isn't chosen. It's created. It's Forged.* |

REALITY CHECK: Circadian Lighting
They have incredible technology, developed so astronauts could operate in space in normal day/night rhythms. Their FORCE was that artificial light ruins a person's ability to operate effectively. Their FRAME demanded precise sunlight wavelength in every light.

When combining their FORCE and FRAME, the inevitable outcome emerged: "Think Brighter."

Schools don't buy circadian lighting. But everyone buys kids who naturally perform better. Factories don't buy circadian lighting. But everyone buys accuracy in the workplace. Hospitals don't buy circadian lighting. But everyone buys quicker healing patients.

Your one thing is built, not picked. It's Forged.

Brands often try to choose their memorable thing from what already exists. Your memorable thing emerges when your FORCE and FRAME work together.

Look at the patterns:

Sephora: Their FORCE (everyone deserves to see their potential) + their FRAME (technology removes guesswork, transformation over transaction) = "I don't just shop there. They make me see my best self."
As a referee: My FORCE (fair game for everyone) + my FRAME (authority, empathy, consistency under pressure) = "Be the referee that teams want on their game."

The memorable thing is Forged through systematic alignment. Through connecting the strings.

Forgetting is automatic.
Learning Guild research on the forgetting curve shows **humans forget 50% of new information within an hour. After 24 hours, we've forgotten 70%. After a week? We're down to about 10%.**[7]

But emotional experiences? Those hold.
Not the details, but the feeling.

That's why your one thing can't be functional. "Great customer service" isn't memorable because everyone claims to offer great customer service. "The place that made me feel like they actually cared" is memorable because most places don't.

Your FRAME is Forging your one thing.
Right now, your FRAME is constructing the foundation for the one thing that will hijack memory. But you won't see what it is until your FUNCTION brings it to life.

The Memory Hierarchy
Works in order:
1. How you made them feel.
2. What you helped them accomplish.
3. What you actually did.
4. What you said you'd do.

99% of brands focus on #4. Smart brands own #1.

Your Belief and Principle aren't just decision-making tools. They're the architecture for something memorable.

When you move into FUNCTION, you'll see how your FORCE and FRAME create inevitable outcomes that competitors can't replicate.

Because in a world where everyone's distracted and overwhelmed, being forgettable is the only unforgivable sin.

Your one thing is being Forged right now.

When it's complete, it becomes the reason people would search for you. Not your products. Not your services. You.

FRAME FORGED BRAND LAW

Every memorable brand has that one thing that's **Forged**.

YOUR FRAME FORGED FIELD TEST

1. **How does your FORCE + FRAME create something inevitable?**
   What emerges when the problem you're fixing meets your Belief and Principle?

2. **What's the feeling people remember after working with you?**
   Not what you did, but how you made them feel about themselves.

3. **If competitors copied everything you do, what couldn't they replicate?**
   That thing they can't fake, that's your one thing.

LESS IS MORE

Instead of optimizing 20 touchpoints, you're perfecting one. You eliminated the pressure to be remarkable at everything.
Your customer experience just got laser-focused.

BRAND STRING THEORY

INTERNAL FUNCTION

Brands aren't born visible.
You build them.
Your FUNCTION.
This is intentional friction.

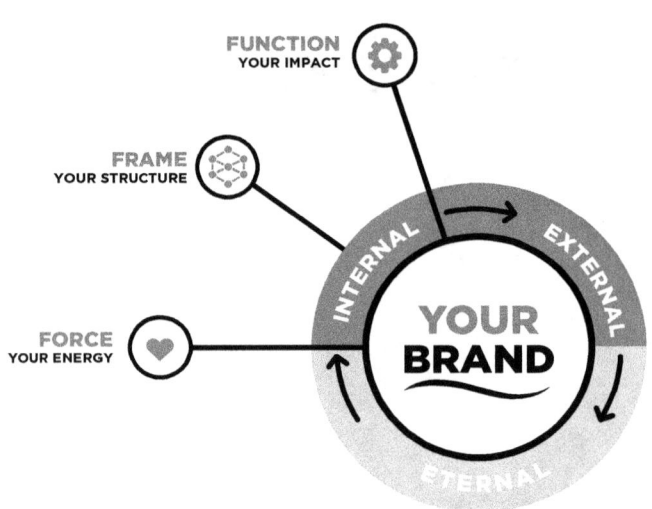

BRAND STRING THEORY

CHAPTER SEVEN
FUNCTION POSITION

IS YOUR BRAND POSITION ALIGNED?

Your brand FORCE gives you purpose. Your FRAME gives you structure. Your FUNCTION is where intention meets reality.

This is where you choose to place your bets and focus your attention. Where you show up isn't a marketing decision. It's the external consequence of what you believe.

This is where your internal brand strategy either works in the real world or falls apart completely.

Your FRAME determines where you can credibly Position yourself. Your Position must align with your FRAME, or the strings break.

| *Position follows FRAME.* |

Brands typically show up everywhere and nowhere simultaneously. They're on Instagram posting motivational quotes, on LinkedIn sharing industry insights, and sending emails about "exciting updates" that excite exactly no one. They mistake presence for strategy.

Space and time are connected. You can't be in the right place at the wrong time and expect anything meaningful to happen.

Position and timing work the same way. They're connected forces that determine if you'll be there when it matters.

Refereeing professional rugby revealed that Positioning is everything. There's only one referee with 30 players. You can't cover every inch of the field. But you can be in the right place at the right moment, moving early and arriving before the action develops. The key isn't just being where something happens. You need to anticipate where it will happen and get there first. When your rhythm and timing is off, you miss critical moments.

And the same applies to your brand.

REALITY CHECK: Supermarket Chain Flower Store
A high-end grocer wanted to add an in-store florist brand. They needed a name, and positioning that would make flowers an attraction, not an afterthought.

Instead of competing with every florist in town across every channel, we focused on one thing: Making the flowers the heroes of the space. Branded in olive and black, the flowers became the focal point that drew customers deeper into the store. The positioning was simple: "This isn't just grocery shopping; it's curating your life." The result was successfully implemented across multiple stores. Customers specifically visited for the experience. The flowers didn't need to be everywhere or in every location, they needed to own one experience.

Salesforce found that **76% of consumers expect consistent interactions across departments, platforms, and devices.**[8] But here's what they didn't mention: "Consistency" doesn't mean "conformity."

Your brand should feel the same wherever customers encounter it, but it doesn't need to be everywhere. Position operates at two levels: the strategic space you claim, and the tactical touchpoints where customers encounter you.

Touchpoints aren't channels, they're proof.

Your FRAME determines both.

The presence problem is that Position without FRAME is just presence. And presence without strategy is pointless. Companies who get it right:

Volvo
Belief: Safety isn't optional.
Principle: Engineered for survival.
Forged: The safe car.
Strategic Position: Family safety vehicle market.
Where They Show Up: Crash test ratings, safety engineering showcases, family SUV segments, IIHS Top Safety Pick awards.

They cannot Position themselves in thrill-seeking performance spaces, because their FRAME won't allow it.

Costco
Belief: Simplicity builds clarity.
Principle: We trust you.
Forged: Shopping without anxiety.
Strategic Position: High-volume simplified retail.
Where They Show Up: Warehouse locations, limited products (4,000 vs. 30,000), membership-only access, trust-based returns.

They can't position in boutique or luxury retail, because their FRAME demands high-volume simplicity.

Monzo
Belief: Banking should be transparent.
Principle: Show everything, hide nothing.
Forged: The honest bank.
Strategic Position: Transparent digital banking.
Where They Show Up: Real-time app notifications, instant spending breakdowns, clear fee structures, no-branch digital experience.

They can't position in traditional branches with complex products, because their FRAME forces digital clarity.

Your strategic Position determines where you must show up.

Volvo can't just claim safety, they must position themselves in crash test leadership, engineering content, and every touchpoint that proves it.

Miss those touchpoints and your Position collapses.

When Position fights FRAME
Traditional positioning treats this as a strategic choice, asking: "What position should we own? What market category? What competitive differentiation?"

You don't choose your Position, your FRAME does.

JCPenney tried to reposition from discount family department store to aspirational boutique experience. They eliminated sales and coupons, the very things their customers valued. Their new Position contradicted their FRAME of accessible value. Revenue dropped almost a billion in one year. When Position fights your FRAME, the string snaps.

Here's how you know if your brand is showing up strategically:
Your Position reinforces your FRAME.
You're part of the conversation as it unfolds.
Your brand can be described the same on three different touchpoints.

Businesses just show up everywhere and wonder why nothing sticks, because they've never asked if their Position aligns with their FRAME.

Position isn't where you want to be.

It's where your FRAME directs you.

Be positioned where your FRAME demands.

FUNCTION POSITION BRAND LAW

Align your **Position** and own the space.

YOUR FUNCTION POSITION FIELD TEST

1. **Where do your customers find you (not where you think they should)?**
   Tests if you understand where your FRAME actually Positions you.

2. **Are you Positioned where your customers are going, or where they've already been?**
   Tests if you're anticipating opportunities or chasing them.

3. **What touchpoint, if removed tomorrow, would actually hurt your business?**
   Separate essential presence from nice-to-have presence.

LESS IS MORE

You stopped spreading yourself thin and started showing up focused. You eliminated the need to be everywhere and started owning spaces that matter.

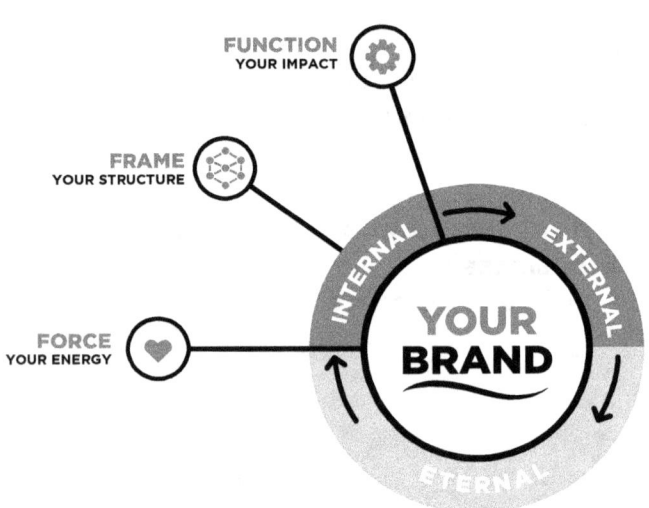

BRAND STRING THEORY

CHAPTER EIGHT
FUNCTION WORKS

WHEN YOUR BRAND WORKS, WHAT DO PEOPLE DO?

In practice, brands measure success by vanity metrics. Likes, followers, impressions, brand awareness.

You know your brand Works when people change their behavior because of it. Not when they see you, but when they act differently because you exist.

The behavior you create is the only metric that matters. I see this all the time working with brands that get excited about engagement rates. They're measuring applause while their business stagnates.

It's great having a packed dancefloor one night, but it needs to be repeated consistently to be a valid metric.

REALITY CHECK: Women's College Rugby Association
They needed to establish themselves as a legitimate FORCE working toward making rugby a recognized NCAA sport. The challenge wasn't awareness, as people knew rugby existed. The challenge was changing how people thought about rugby's place in American college athletics. The rebrand positioned them not as "just another sports organization," but as the definitive pathway for rugby to join the NCAA family.

We focused on the behaviors that would prove legitimacy, which has increased university participation, and standardized rugby competition structures within the US landscape. Since the rebrand, they've been steadily growing toward their NCAA goal. Universities are adding programs, athletes are choosing rugby over other sports, and most importantly, athletics directors are taking meetings they wouldn't take before.

The brand Works because it changed what people do, not just what they think.

Research from Buyapowa shows that **88% of consumers trust word of mouth from friends and family over brand messaging.**[9] It means that when your brand Works, your customers become your marketing department. But this only happens when you give them something worth talking about.

The Action Hierarchy
Not all customer actions are created equal. Here's how to recognize when your brand is actually working:

Level 1: Compliance: Customers do what you ask them to do. Fill out the form, make the purchase, download the app. This is table stakes.

Level 2: Preference: They choose you when they have options. This means your brand is working at a basic level. You've created enough differentiation to win in a comparison.

Level 3: Advocacy: They recommend you without being asked. They naturally bring your brand into conversations. This is where many brands want to be, but few achieve this.

Level 4: Identity: They incorporate your brand into their identity. They don't just use your product; they identify with what it represents. This is rare and powerful.

Level 5: Defense: They defend your brand when others criticize it. They feel personally invested in your success. This is the holy grail.

Most brands optimize for Level 1 and wonder why their growth stagnates. Smart brands design for Level 3 and above.

The Behavior Diagnostic
Purchase Patterns: Are people buying once or buying repeatedly? Are they upgrading, expanding, or just replacing? The pattern tells you if your brand is working or if you're just convenient.

Sharing Behavior: What do people share about you, and how do they share it? Do they post pictures? Do they tag friends? Do they tell stories? The type of sharing reveals the depth of connection.

Word-of-Mouth Quality: When people recommend you, what do they say? Do they explain features or do they describe outcomes? Do they sound like your marketing copy or do they use their own words?

Keeping vs. Finding Customers: Are you growing because existing customers stay longer and do more, or because you're constantly finding new customers to replace ones who leave? The ratio tells you everything about brand strength.

REALITY CHECKS:
Airbnb: Level 4: Identity
They never asked customers to post photos of their stays. They did it anyway. Because staying in an Airbnb didn't feel like lodging. It felt like belonging. Identity, not transaction. When a brand makes people feel like they're part of something bigger, sharing becomes instinctive, not incentivized.

Oura Ring: Level 3: Obsession
Oura Ring users don't just wear the ring. They become biometric nerds, sharing sleep scores in the app's "Circles" feature, comparing recovery data, and building rituals around their metrics. Behavior driven by self-optimization. They don't just use the product, they let it shape their routines.

Lush: Level 2: Performance
Lush customers film themselves using bath bombs, create tutorials, and proudly display their hauls on social media. They turned personal care into performance because the brand makes them feel both creative and ethical. That's Level 2. Behavior as self-expression.

Slack: Level 4: Identity
Slack users aren't just messaging. They're making custom emojis, building elaborate channels, and introducing Slack to new teams. It's not "the company uses Slack." It's "We are a Slack team" vs. an email team. That's Level 4 behavior, not tool behavior.

Notice that none of these brands are asking people to share. They've created experiences worth sharing. There's a difference.

The Multiplier Effect
When your brand really Works, customer behavior creates more customers without additional effort from you. This is when you know you've built something sustainable.

Learned behavior can also be negative. I discovered this the hard way with my son Sam. When he was very young, he asked me a this-or-that question and I sarcastically answered, "Yes." The shock on his face meant eternal revenge. Now, he's an adult, and when I ask him anything, (even "What are you doing?"), he'll answer "YES." One moment of sarcasm created a permanent behavioral pattern.

Brands work the same way. Every interaction teaches customers how to interact with you next time.

But here's what most companies miss. The behavior you want to create must align with the behavior your brand naturally encourages. You can't force people to share if your experience isn't share-worthy. You can't create advocates if you're not advocacy-worthy.

As a rugby referee, I learned that it's not about me, it's about the game. Players start defending your calls when they trust your judgment.

| *Respect isn't demanded, it's consistently earned.* |

With brands, word-of-mouth often happens organically when customers trust that your success aligns with their success.

Build something that your customers and clients will defend.

FUNCTION WORKS BRAND LAW

When your brand **Works**, people don't just buy, they belong.

YOUR FUNCTION WORKS FIELD TEST

1. **What do your best customers do that average consumers don't?**
   Look for patterns in behavior, not just demographics or purchase amounts.

2. **How do people discover you (their behavior, not your marketing)?**
   Track actual discovery paths, referrals, searches, and word-of-mouth.

3. **What do people do differently because your brand exists?**
   Look for behavior changes you create, not just compliance or transactions.

LESS IS MORE

You stopped optimizing for vanity metrics and started measuring what actually matters. Your success just became predictable instead of random.

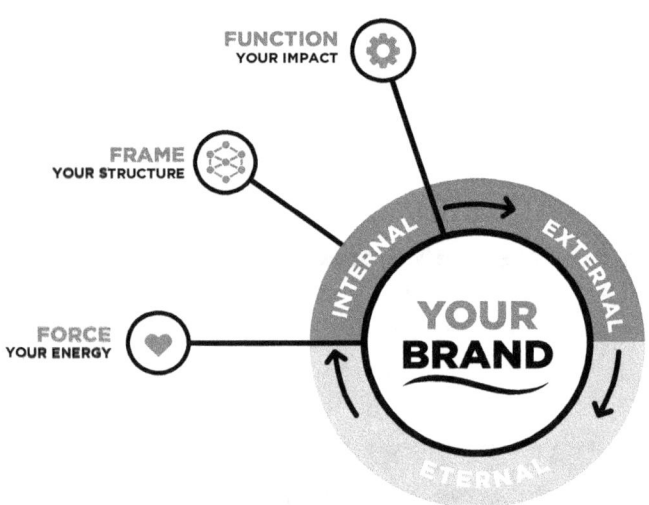

BRAND STRING THEORY

CHAPTER NINE
FUNCTION FRICTION

YOUR CUSTOMER JOURNEY DELIVERS FRICTION. GOOD OR BAD?

Every brand has a breaking point. That moment where the experience goes from smooth to frustrating, where trust turns to doubt, where customers choose to bail or stick around.

So many brands don't know where their breaking point is. They never honestly look for it. They optimize for the good bits and ignore the fragile parts until customers complain.

Teradata found that **32% of customers will walk away from a brand they love after a single bad experience.**[10] Think about that. One bad experience can undo years of good. Finding your Friction points isn't just important, it's survival.

I learned this lesson many times over, and you may have too. In any relationship, you have to be honest and consistent, because if you're not, small frustrations can build until the facade cracks, and you are not who you said you were.

The same thing happens with brands. They might handle the big moments well; the purchase, the delivery, the major interactions. But they miss the small Friction points that accumulate until customers reach their breaking point.

| *Understanding Friction is about making things clearer.* |

Is all Friction bad?
Almost all brands think Friction is always bad. Friction can be strategic. **Apple** makes you jump through hoops to get support, but they do it in a way that feels premium, not frustrating. The Genius Bar appointment system ensures quality support that builds brand trust. And if you've used it, it's exciting and packed with anticipation.

Even if they say your device is dead forever, it's okay. Everyone gave it their best shot. And the outcome feels Frictionless.

Then there's two-factor authentication. Pain in the ass? Yes. Protects everyone? Also yes.

My wife Anna designs for how people actually move and live in spaces, not just how her buildings look in photos. She creates deliberate contrast. Intentional Friction. Materials that transition from smooth to rough. A lower ceiling which leads to a room that lifts up to the sky. A narrow passageway to open green spaces. "The lungs of the house," as she puts it. She guides people naturally toward the experiences that matter most. Your brand should guide people the same way. The design is intentional.

IKEA makes you build it yourself. You hate it during, love it after. The effort creates ownership.

Alinea in Chicago makes you prepay for your meal when you book, and reservations open at specific times like concert tickets. The Friction makes it feel like an event, not just dinner.

Ask
"Does this Friction protect value or make things harder?" If it protects value, quality, security, and service, it's strategic. If it just makes things harder because you haven't fixed your process, it's destructive.

Hiut Denim forge the best jeans through "craft over everything," with a principle that delivers GrandMaster craftsmanship in every pair, but their "no growth" policy delivered exclusive friction, until demand forced them to rework their approach. Their new ownership has pledged to honor their beliefs and principles, knowing it takes 3 years to train a Grandmaster. With a solid foundation, their story is one worth following.

REALITY CHECK: Trader Joe's
They have strategic Friction everywhere. Limited selection (FRAME Forged: Curated not comprehensive). No online shopping (FUNCTION Works: In-store discovery). No sales or coupons (FRAME Principle: Everyday value). Every Friction point is built from their internal engine and it reinforces who they are. Competitors can't copy it without becoming them.

As a referee, the best matches are the ones where no one mentions or thinks about the referee. The same applies to brands. The best customer experiences are the ones where people barely notice the process, they just focus on the outcome.

| *Your best performances may go unnoticed, but they're memorable.* |

Fans remember the game. Fans remember your brand.

Major League Baseball sponsorship revenue hit $2.05 billion in 2025, up 68% since 2022. The 2025 World Series averaged 34 million viewers with game 7 hitting 51 million, the largest global audience in 34 years. What changed? Baseball removed destructive friction. Pitch clock killed dead time. Eliminating defensive shifts restored action. Limiting mound visits kept momentum. Purists complained, but revenue rose because MLB stopped protecting rituals and started protecting attention.

Your customers aren't asking you to transform everything. They're asking you to remove the Friction that makes engagement feel like work, and to be intentional about the Friction you create. Brands worth searching for don't make things easy. They make the right things inevitable.

Design Friction that serves your brand.

FUNCTION FRICTION BRAND LAW

Balance **Friction** to deliver the best outcomes.

YOUR FUNCTION FRICTION FIELD TEST

1. **Where do your customers struggle, hesitate, or give up?**
   Map actual problem points in your customer journey, not assumed ones.

2. **What Friction protects your brand?**
   Identify strategic Friction.

3. **What would break if you doubled your customer volume tomorrow?**
   Identify systems that work now but won't scale, your hidden Friction points.

LESS IS MORE

You stopped letting Friction happen to you and started making it work for you. You eliminated the bad Friction and kept what builds value. Your customer experience just became intentional.

INTERNAL CASE STUDIES
WEWORK

WeWork convinced the world that real estate was tech and hit $47 billion. They thought they had FORCE: "Changing how the world works" and killing long-term leases. But this was their tagline masquerading as their FORCE.

As my son Sam asked: "Are you lying for attention?" That's exactly what WeWork did. They fell in love with grand messaging instead of fixing what was actually broken.

They changed nothing. Coworking had existed since forever. WeWork became Regus with kombucha. The disaster was: No FRAME. No Principle. No Discipline.

They expanded everywhere, said yes to everything, and couldn't decide if they were tech or a landlord. When you stand for everything, you stand for nothing. Zero Friction meant members could join and leave easily, while WeWork carried serious long-term leases.

Back when they started, the fix could have been profit-share deals with landlords. Prime metros only with 70%+ pre-sold before expansion. Pricing ladder for longer commitments. Tech workspaces people fight to stay in.

And learning to say no.

What they did.

WEWORK INTERNAL

	FORCE	
WORTH	✘	"We're changing how the world works."
CHANGE	✘	Zero. Regus with a whistle and a bell.
DISAPPEARED	✓	Long-term leases would not be obsolete.
	FRAME	
BELIEF	✘	No operational decision-making belief.
PRINCIPLE	✘	No "won't factor." Said yes to everything.
FORGED	✘	Workspace? Tech company? Real estate company?
	FUNCTION	
POSITION	✘	Turned up everywhere without strategy.
WORKS	✓	People changed how they work.
FRICTION	✘	Easy to join, equally easy to leave.

What they could've done.

WEWORK INTERNAL FIX

	FORCE	
WORTH	✓	Long-term leases are inflexible and expensive.
CHANGE	✓	Profit-sharing deals with landlords eliminate risk.
DISAPPEARED	✓	Long-term leases would not be obsolete.
	FRAME	
BELIEF	✓	Occupancy before expansion.
PRINCIPLE	✓	Flexible space without long-term risk.
FORGED	✓	Tech workspaces that build community.
	FUNCTION	
POSITION	✓	Flexible metro workspaces.
WORKS	✓	People change how they work.
FRICTION	✓	Easy to join, minimal commitment unlocks value.

APPLE INTERNAL

FORCE

WORTH ✓ Technology is intimidating and complex.
They removed the need to think about how technology works.

CHANGE ✓ Technology should feel human.
Didn't compete on specs and built something only they could.

DISAPPEARED ✓ Seamless digital ecosystems would be gone.
They're not everything to everyone but essential to many.

FRAME

BELIEF ✓ Intuitive design isn't negotiable.
Every decision is filtered through one belief, their yes/no machine: Intuition.

PRINCIPLE ✓ "Less is more" always delivers.
Stopped chasing features, owned a Principle that delivered quality hardware and software.

FORGED ✓ Making premium feel simple.
They perfected one truth: Simplicity.

FUNCTION

POSITION ✓ Experience-first retail.
Consolidated presence and built temples.

WORKS ✓ Customers as brand evangelists.
Started measuring passion and belonging.

FRICTION ✓ High price, premium value.
Stopped fearing high prices by delivering exclusive value.

Apple was just another computer company. Beige boxes fighting on specs. When Jobs returned in 1997, he didn't invent something new. He reasserted a principle that changed everything. Technology should feel human, not intimidating.

Most of the industry accepted complexity as inevitable. Manuals, learning curves, frustration. Jobs refused. His FORCE: Technology was a barrier. Apple's mission was to make it usable.

This wasn't about being different. It was about fixing what was broken. Apple's FRAME became their competitive weapon.

Every decision filtered through one belief: That intuitive design isn't negotiable. If something required explanation, it was cut.

Their PRINCIPLE separated them permanently from competitors. While others added buttons and options, Apple simplified. The headphone jack. DVD drives. Ports. Each removal felt reckless to the industry, but obvious to Apple.

The result? Making complex technology work and feel simple became their Forged identity. Not chosen in a strategy session but inevitable from their internal engine.

FUNCTION followed naturally. Experience-first retail stores where you touch products before buying. Premium pricing that filters for believers, not bargain hunters. Loyal customers who not only purchase the product, but also evangelize it.

Apple's strings connect: Broken technology + design obsession = seamless experience. Competitors copy their look but miss their conviction. They can't fake the principle that drives every choice.

When your FORCE and FRAME align this clearly, external success is predictable. Apple didn't just build better computers; they proved technology could feel human. That now drives a trillion-dollar ecosystem competitors still can't replicate.

The lesson: Your internal engine determines everything external. Get the strings connected, and success follows the pattern.

100+ YEARS IN MANUFACTURING

They came to me with their tagline, "Innovators in Lighting." Much like every other lighting company. What would happen if they disappeared tomorrow? Someone else would fill the orders.

That's the problem. After a century in business, they'd become replaceable.

They don't sell lights. They enable critical work in technical spaces where precision, safety, and compliance are non-negotiable.

Failure is not an option.

Built on that internal engine, I repositioned them to "Illuminating Your World." They sell outcomes, not parts: A visual identity that read clean and precise, through deliberate color choices, a refreshed mark (that stayed recognizable), and typography that read "We know what we're doing."

Now they light rooms where lives are on the line, where food processing feeds families, and spaces where futures are built. Now they own the environments where precision, safety, and advancement matter most.

Result: They moved from competing purely on price to strategic partnerships with consistently higher margins.

That's what happens when your INTERNAL engine is clear. You stop being replaceable and start being essential.

MANUFACTURER INTERNAL

FORCE

WORTH Critical spaces demand zero failure.

Enables applications where precision, safety, and compliance are non-negotiable.

CHANGE Future-proof applications with technical subject-matter expertise.

Luminaires that perform in the spaces they serve today and tomorrow.

DISAPPEARED Technical spaces lose a trusted standard.

The partner for environments where risk is eliminated.

FRAME

BELIEF Where specification meets application.

Quotes, parts, engineering, production, marketing, etc. Every decision protects the application.

PRINCIPLE Illuminating mission-critical spaces.

Not fixtures. Not lighting solutions. Luminaires for environments where failure isn't an option.

FORGED Peace of mind, backed by a century of certified performance.

When you're trusted for over a 100 years, you set the standard.

FUNCTION

POSITION The standard from specifier to building owner.

Chosen in design, defended in submittals, trusted by owners.

WORKS ✓ Strategic partner, default specification.

Transition from vendor to trusted partner.

FRICTION ✓ Higher bar, fewer failures.

The discipline that delivers certification is the same discipline that eliminates call-backs.

Where your brand meets the world.
EXTERNAL

CONCEPT
CONNECT
CONVERT

BRAND STRING THEORY

EXTERNAL CONCEPT

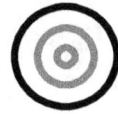

A few seconds can break your brand.
You build it.
Your CONCEPT.
Your millisecond survival strategy.

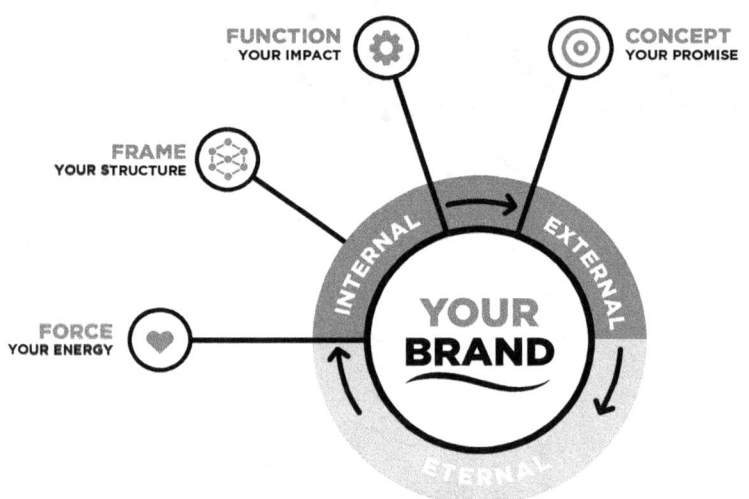

BRAND STRING THEORY

CHAPTER TEN
CONCEPT HOOK

THE REAL HOOK.
WHO ARE YOU TALKING TO?

Your customers aren't just buying your product or service. They're buying how it makes them feel about themselves, their business, and their future. But first, you need to know who you're talking to and discover the feeling behind the FUNCTION, the Hook.

REALITY CHECK: Hazardous Location Manufacturer
They sell specialized products for hazardous locations. Oil rigs, chemical plants, mining operations. Technical specs matter, but that's not what drives decisions.

Hazardous Location ratings are complex, and most people in the industry can't explain their way around the classes, divisions, zones, groups, and temperatures, nor what they actually mean. Their breakthrough came when we created a "Hazardous Location Guide" infographic, that became their most-shared content. Visually simplified technical expertise built trust.

But here's what really happened: Everyone involved in the selection and purchasing process felt confident they were making the right choice.

| **The emotion isn't excitement or happiness. It's relief.** |

Research from Google and CEB's Marketing Leadership Council found that **B2B buyers are 50% more likely to purchase when they see personal value (such as career advancement or confidence in their choice) and are 8x more likely to pay a premium when personal value is present.**[11] People don't just buy what you sell; they buy how it makes them feel.

Most companies chase the wrong emotions.

They think everyone wants to feel "excited" or "inspired."

The corporate examples everyone knows (consumer brands selling feelings directly) are:
Coca-Cola: Happiness and togetherness.
Nike: Motivation and achievement.
LEGO: Creativity and imagination.

Deeper emotional Hooks are often quieter:
Relief: Finally, someone who gets it.
Confidence: I'm making the smart choice.
Vindication: I knew this was the right approach.
Security: This won't come back to haunt me.

Examples are:
Relief: **TurboTax**.
"Taxes, done smarter" is what users feel. Relief from the anxiety of tax season thanks to clear guidance and a sense that the software meets all their needs.

Confidence: **Uniqlo.**
The Japanese basic clothing retailer said, "Quality basics for everyone." Fashion is traditionally divided into luxury or disposable. Uniqlo's Hook: Confidence that functional clothing is accessible regardless of budget.

Vindication: **Whole Foods**.
Longtime shoppers who prioritized organic or ethical sourcing now see mainstream adoption and media validation. Their choice was "right all along."

Security: **ADT**.
"I'm always protected." Homeowners know their investment in security systems buys peace of mind; they won't have to regret "what if?"

| B2C emotions are about how they feel. |

| B2B emotions are about career advancement. |

In B2B, smart choices make everyone look good. They're not just putting their trust in you; they are putting their life on the line for you.

Identifying who this is for and what they're feeling, leads into your headline.

Your Hook attracts, delivers, and empowers. It's about talking directly to the right people. It delivers clarity and empowers them to self-select: "This is me," or "This isn't for me."

Now you understand the responsibility you have.

Your real emotional Hook:
What do you want people to feel first when they encounter your brand?

Not what sounds impressive.

What outcome matches what your product provides.

If you solve expensive problems, they should feel relief.
If you provide expertise, they should feel confident.

If you simplify complexity, they should feel smart.

Emotion drives everything.

Find it first.

CONCEPT HOOK BRAND LAW

Your **Hook** attracts, delivers, and empowers.

YOUR CONCEPT HOOK FIELD TEST

1. **Who are you talking to, and what are they feeling?**
   Identify who they are and what they feel. Frustrated? Confused? Overwhelmed?

2. **What do you want them to feel when they encounter your brand?**
   Relief? Confidence? Vindication? Security?

3. **What lasting emotion should your brand leave behind?**
   The personal value they defend, retell, and build trust on.

LESS IS MORE

Most companies chase excitement or inspiration. You found who you're talking to and the emotion that matters, protects careers, and builds trust. Everything else follows from there.

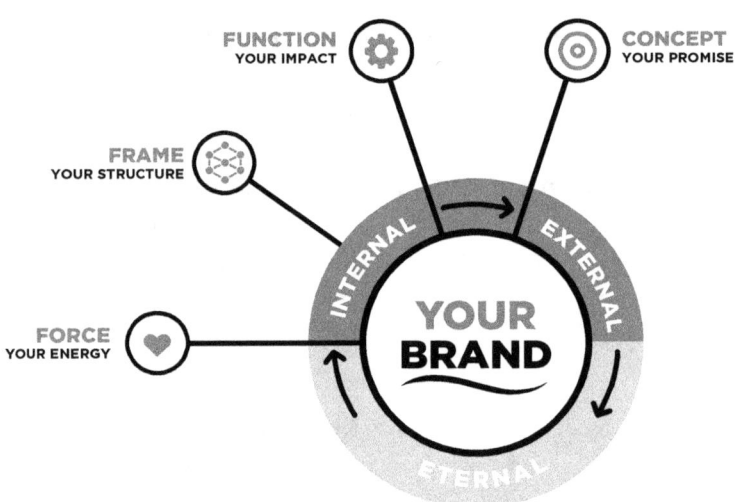

BRAND STRING THEORY

CHAPTER ELEVEN
CONCEPT SENTENCE

YOUR BRAND HAS ONLY ONE SENTENCE TO LIVE BY. WHAT DOES IT SAY?

This is where your internal brand strategy meets the real world.

Your Sentence isn't hidden in an internal document or buried on your "About" page.

This is your tagline.
Your homepage hero.
Your landing page headline.

The first words people see when they encounter your brand.

Some brands try to say everything and end up saying nothing. They write mission statements for internal meetings, then wonder why their marketing doesn't convert. They craft beautiful brand strategies that never make it to the customer.

Your Sentence is your most important piece of external communication.

| One Sentence ensures clarity never leaves the room. |

You know those moments when you feel the pressure to deliver the succinct, ground-breaking message, but you just can't help stumbling over your tongue and back again?

It happens to all of us.

In refereeing rugby, you have so little time to explain a call, unless you want to explain how right you are. If you can't communicate in a straightforward and easy to understand way, you've lost the players. It takes preparation. Know what you're going to say, and how you're going to say it.

Use your words.

Make your value clear in one breath, or lose the customer. Your external value in one Sentence.

REALITY CHECK: PR Firm
They led with awards. All of them. "Brand Marketer of the Year." "Firm of the Year Finalist." "Global PR Campaign Finalist." Stevies, Bulldog Awards, AMA distinctions. Enough trophies to fill a lobby.
Their homepage read like a resume. A wall of logos, headlines, and press clippings. Top 3 Brand Marketer in the U.S. Blog posts about being "mesmerized" by their clients' products.

But when you stripped all that away, here's what they actually did:
They made unknown brands show up everywhere.

ESPN. CNN. Wall Street Journal. USA Today. New York Times. Chicago Tribune. San Francisco Chronicle. Consumer products that had no right being in major media... suddenly were. A first-season MMA promotion on national TV. A startup gadget competing with Logitech in the same headlines. A private jet company showing up in mainstream business press.

They didn't do "Public Relations and Marketing Communications."

They made invisible brands visible.

Their line should've been:
"We Make Unknown Brands Impossible to Ignore."

Instead, they chose awards over clarity.

When you have one moment, do you choose Mirror Guy, go on safari, or tell them what they get?

The brutal truth is this:

| **Paying attention is free. Missing the moment is not.** |

When someone encounters your brand, they're making a split-second decision. Miss that moment, and you've lost more than a customer, you've lost a relationship that could have lasted years. Your Craigslist missed connection. Your one Sentence isn't marketing copy, it's what makes them decide to pay attention.

Think about it. When you meet someone new, you form an opinion in seconds. Maybe less. It may not be accurate, but in your mind, in that moment, it's completely valid. Your one Sentence is your survival strategy.

Don't optimize for impressiveness. Center clarity.
If your goal is to sound sophisticated, comprehensive, and innovative, you end up sounding like everyone else.

The Sentence Test
Your first Sentence is what the world sees first. Your external promise.

Patagonia: "Save our home planet."
That's it. Not "We create high-quality outdoor gear for adventure enthusiasts who value sustainability and performance." To understand their tagline, their FORCE was the frustration that business and environmental protection were seen as opposites.
Slack: "Where work happens."
Not "We provide enterprise communication solutions that integrate seamlessly with existing workflows." Their FORCE was the frustration that work communication was scattered, inefficient, and siloed. They make work better. Period.
Headspace: "Be kind to your mind."
Not "We deliver evidence-based mindfulness solutions through accessible digital meditation experiences." They help you be kind to your mind. Frustration that mental wellness was complicated, clinical, and inaccessible, was their FORCE.

Notice what these taglines have in common? They're about the customer, not the company. They focus on the outcome, not the process. They use words humans actually say.

Your one Sentence adapts. But your core Sentence expresses differently across touchpoints:

TAGLINES that capture who you are:
• Dollar Shave Club: "Great razors for a few bucks a month."
HOMEPAGE headlines that explain what you deliver:
• Calendly: "Easy scheduling ahead."
LANDING PAGES that promise what they'll accomplish:
• Later: "Instagram influencer marketing strategy guide."

Ads that challenge what they think:
• Blissy: "It's not a pillowcase. It's a beauty treatment."
Same core truth. Different expressions for different moments in the customer journey.

Most Sentences fail for predictable reasons:
They're about you, not them: "We are a leading provider of..." Nobody cares that you think you're leading.

They list capabilities: "We provide comprehensive solutions including..." Capabilities don't motivate action. Outcomes do.

They use industry jargon: "Leveraging synergistic methodologies..." If your grandparents and your kids can't understand it, it's not clear enough. They try to include everyone: "For businesses of all sizes..." When you're for everyone, you're for no one.

They hedge their bets: "We help enable organizations to potentially..." Confidence is clarity. Wishy-washy language creates wishy-washy results.

Finding your Sentence:
Start with the problem: What keeps your customers up all night? That's what you solve.
Focus on the outcome: What does life look like after they work with you? That's what you deliver.
Use their language: How do your best customers describe what you do? Use their words, not yours.
Test for clarity: Can someone who's never heard of your industry understand it? If not, simplify.

Make it decisive: Choose one thing you do better than anyone else.

Own that.

The Ripple Effect
When you nail your one Sentence, everything else gets easier:
- Sales conversations start with the problem you solve, not the services you offer.
- Marketing messages focus on customer outcomes, not company capabilities.
- Hiring decisions attract people who believe in you, not just a paycheck.
- Partnership opportunities align around shared customer value, not shared features.
- Pricing conversations justify value through transformation, not time.
- Your Sentence becomes the filter for every message. Does this support what you promise? If yes, say it. If no, don't.

Your brand's one Sentence (whether it's a tagline or a headline), is built on your internal FORCE, FRAME, and FUNCTION.

Everything should be connected.

Now connect everything.

CONCEPT SENTENCE **BRAND LAW**

Keep clarity in the room with one **Sentence** that solves and delivers.

YOUR **CONCEPT SENTENCE** FIELD TEST

1. **What problem keeps your best customers up all night?**
   Start with their suffering, not your solution.

2. **Does your sentence make people want to pay attention?**
   Share it with someone who doesn't know your business. Do they ask "Tell me more" or "So what?"

3. **If you could only do one thing for the rest of your business life, what would it be?**
   That's probably your sentence.

LESS IS MORE

You eliminated the need to explain everything and started talking about what matters.
Your marketing just invited attention to meet clarity.

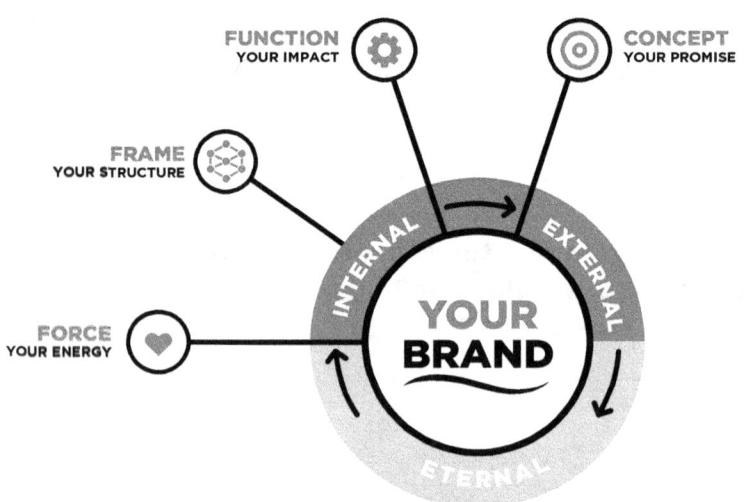

BRAND STRING THEORY

CHAPTER TWELVE
CONCEPT TODAY

IS YOUR MESSAGE RELEVANT TODAY, OR YESTERDAY?

Every brand is haunted by its greatest hits.

Your brand isn't static. Your business isn't the same as it was three years ago. It may not even be the same as it was three months ago.

But your messaging? Is that still talking about who you used to be.

This is the curse of successful brands. They find something that works, and stick with it long past its expiration date. It becomes a museum of your former self while your competitors talk about the future.

Museum brands. Beautiful, silent, and empty.

Paid your Blockbuster late fees recently? Found your Sears credit card? Developed your Kodak film?

Research reveals a stark disconnect: PwC, cited in The Relevance Group report in 2023 that **90% of executives believe their brand is trusted by customers, while only 30% of business-to-customers agree.**[12.1] **Business-to-business is down to 14%** according to Forrester. [12.2] Meanwhile, the EY Global Consumer Report in 2024 shares that **just 12% of consumers feel that brand messaging truly aligns with their values.**[12.3] It shows how brands cling to outdated perceptions of their relevance.

That's not brand consistency. That's brand laziness.

Every industry I've worked in proves this. In refereeing, the game evolves. New laws, new interpretations, new styles of play. If you're still calling the game like it's 2010, you're going nowhere. The best referees adapt while maintaining their core identity.

Being a DJ is the same. You have to read the room and evolve your set while staying true to who you are.

Brands are no different. You evolve.

| *Your message should make your old self proud.* |

The Evolution Problem
Most brands evolve accidentally and communicate intentionally. They change what they do but keep saying what they've always said. This creates a gap between promises and reality that customers notice immediately.

It happens because changing your message feels risky. What if customers liked the old version? What if we lose our identity? What if you confuse people?

But your customers already know you've changed. When your message doesn't match their experience, they don't trust either.

Most brands get stuck echoing who they used to be: "Family-owned since 1985." Most family ownership is irrelevant today. "Local expertise." When you serve customers nationally.
"Handcrafted quality." When you've scaled through better systems.

These aren't false. They're incomplete truths that miss your current reality.

Jaguar just threw away 90 years of British luxury performance for geometric shapes and abstract messaging that could sell anything from NFTs to cold plunges. They were so afraid of looking old that they forgot what made them worth keeping around. Their existing customers feel betrayed, and new customers have no idea why Jaguar exists.

This is what happens when you panic about relevance instead of evolving your message. When this makes your old self proud, you're on the right track.

The Message Evolution Success
Mailchimp proves you can evolve without losing your core. They've grown from a simple email tool to a comprehensive marketing platform over 24 years. However, their messaging stayed true to their positioning: Growing with small businesses.

Their smart evolution:
2009: "We make email marketing easy & fun."
2013: "Send better email."
2017: "Being yourself makes all the difference."
2021: "Get down to business and grow sales."
2025: "Turn emails & SMS into revenue."

What they kept consistent: The focus on accessibility and growth. They never abandoned their "grow with you" promise to chase enterprise messaging (except during the initial Intuit acquisition period around 2021).

The strategic genius: While others target enterprises with high-cost, high-complexity positioning, Mailchimp captures businesses early and keeps them longer. Lower entry cost, higher lifetime value.

The Today Test
What do you do now that you didn't do three years ago?
What problems do you solve now that you couldn't solve before?
If your messaging doesn't reflect these changes, you're echoing.
Your message should grow with your business. The alternative is becoming irrelevant while trying to stay consistent.

There's no need to be a tribute band to your former self.

CONCEPT TODAY BRAND LAW

Your message **Today** should make your old self proud.

YOUR CONCEPT TODAY FIELD TEST

1. **What do you do Today that you couldn't (or didn't) do before?**
   Make sure your messaging reflects your evolved capabilities.

2. **Who are your customers Today vs. who they were before?**
   Update your language to speak to your actual market.

3. **How has your delivery method changed or improved?**
   Don't hide improvements behind outdated messaging.

LESS IS MORE

You stopped being a museum of your former self and started revolving your message with your business. You have become relevant through honest evolution.

EXTERNAL CONNECT

No one falls in love with your brand by accident.
You build it.
Your CONNECT.
Leave a mark, not a moment.

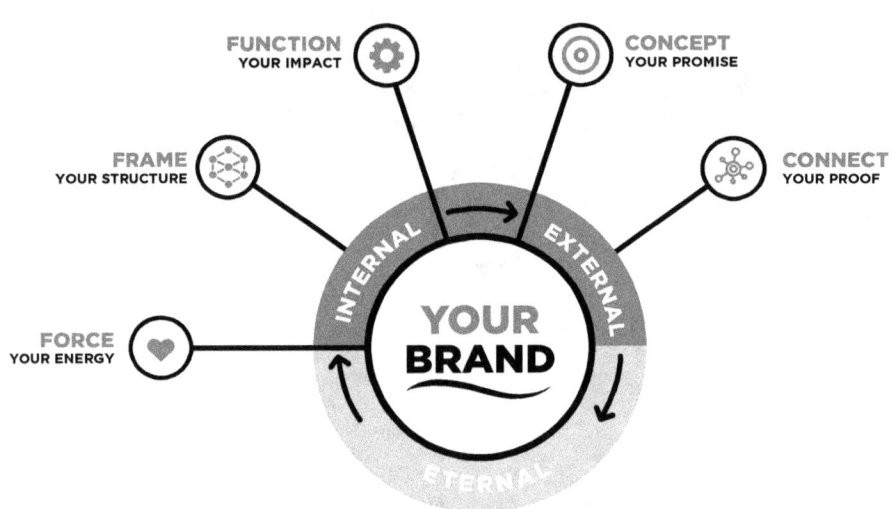

BRAND STRING THEORY

CHAPTER THIRTEEN
CONNECT BENEFITS

BENEFITS SEPARATE YOUR BRAND. DOES YOUR DESIGN BACK IT UP?

Listing Benefits is easy. Making them believable is branding. Your design is the proof that makes them believable.

Every competitor can claim quality, innovation, or customer service. But what specific Benefits do you deliver that others don't, or won't? Those distinctions only work when your design proves they're real.

Brands often list features and hope customers figure out the Benefits. Smart brands lead with the outcomes that separate them, then use every visual element to reinforce why those Benefits are credible.

When your distinctions align with your design, your Benefits feel honest.

| **Competitors can't copy you. They'd have to become you.** |

REALITY CHECK: SPOT Real Estate
They have a business model that makes sense: Full-service real estate for 1% instead of 3%. Simple.

But nobody believes it.

For decades, homeowners had two choices: pay premium commission to a traditional broker, or go barebones with a flat-fee service and figure it out alone. The market called that a spectrum. SPOT calls it a false choice.

The benefit isn't what you save. It's what you finally get: full representation, full service, at a commission rate that should have always been the standard. The system was never broken.

It was just convenient for everyone except the homeowner.

Traditional brokers can't match it.
Flat-fee services can't deliver it.

SPOT: The 1% in Real Estate.

They own the standard.

It's about alignment.

Too many brands don't have a style guide problem. They have a fragmentation problem. Their design says one thing. Their tone says another. Their product promises something else entirely.

United Airlines promised Benefits like "seamless travel experience" and "friendly service," with smiling faces of travelers and airline staff. But, the 2017 passenger-dragging incident and their consistent baggage handling issues make those Benefits impossible to believe. They keep cycling through taglines. "Fly the Friendly Skies," "Connected to the moments that matter," "Good Leads the Way." It's like a cloud came over their Benefits. New messaging can't restore credibility to promises customers have seen violated.

Wells Fargo ensured personalized banking relationships, financial expertise, and homeownership guidance. But their Benefits crumbled under scrutiny. "Personalized service" became fake accounts opened without permission. "Financial expertise" became selling unnecessary insurance to meet quotas. "Homeownership support" became improper foreclosures. The century-old stagecoach branding seemed more like a hold up and a hold out. When your operations systematically violate your promised Benefits, no design can make them believable.

The fragmentation shows the real cost of misalignment:
Your brand becomes easy to ignore.
Or worse... easy to copy.

Brands that present themselves consistently across various platforms are 3-4 times more likely to achieve strong visibility,[13] Renderforest data from 2024 shows.

Visual Alignment = Benefit Clarity
Your design isn't decoration; it's proof. It makes your difference look real. It makes your positioning feel earned. When a prospect sees your site, touches your packaging, or opens your email, they're asking:

"Do I believe this company can deliver what they claim?"
That's what great design answers.

Promise a new future? Look innovative.
Sell simplicity? Strip the extras.
Claim trustworthiness? Every detail must feel intentional.
Offer premium? Your fonts and finish better not be discount.

Because... **Bad fonts read cheap.**
Paul Rand said your font is the silent ambassador of your brand. If your message says "premium" but your font says "amateur," you're forgettable before you even start talking. Every font choice either strengthens your brand or unravels it.

| *Always know why you choose a font.* |

Design isn't just about getting it done, it's about knowing when it's ready, when it's actually good. Does it need further development, or does it need to be pulled back? AI can copy style, but only humans know when the connections are strong enough to matter. Good taste is the difference between a brand that works and a brand that converts.

Good design proves the promise.

Great design makes the promise feel inevitable.

Alignment that can't be copied.

Duolingo: That owl, that cheeky copy, that playful user experience (UX). You can't copy it without becoming it.

Barbour: 130 years of weatherproof expertise shows in every visual element. Their timeless design reinforces durability and heritage without feeling dated. They still hand-manufacture their iconic Bedale and Beaufort jackets in the same Simonside factory, where craftspeople lovingly rewax and repair customers' worn jackets by hand. Their website, their stores, their packaging, everything feels like it was built to last generations, not to chase trends. You can't copy their look without copying their 130-year story.
Braun: The German appliance manufacturer makes every button, every line scream German engineering. Their design proves "less but better" isn't a slogan, it's a religion. Competitors copy the look, miss the obsession.

These brands use design to show what they stand for. Their Benefits feel inevitable before you even read the copy.

Your brand works the same way.

In rugby, players test the referee's consistency, not charisma. One call out of alignment with your tone or logic, and authority disappears.

One off-brand moment can undo a lifetime of credibility. When design, voice, and experience all deliver the same Benefits, trust builds before the pitch even starts.

The Distinction Test

Ask yourself: Would someone who only sees your brand visuals know your Benefits?
Can a competitor steal your look without stealing your soul?
Do your materials reinforce your positioning, or not?

Your alignment isn't about aesthetics.
It's about whether people believe what you say.

Turn your separators into visual proof that sells before you speak.

CONNECT BENEFITS BRAND LAW

Design makes your **Benefits** impossible to miss.

YOUR CONNECT BENEFITS FIELD TEST

1. **What Benefits do you deliver that others don't?**
   Identify your true distinctions, not just your features.

2. **Does your design make those Benefits feel credible and real?**
   Test if your visuals support or undermine your Benefits.

3. **Would someone who only sees your visuals know your Benefits?**
   Ensure your design communicates your differentiators without explanation.

LESS IS MORE

You stopped hoping customers would figure out your Benefits and started making them visible. Your design now works as your sales team 24/7.

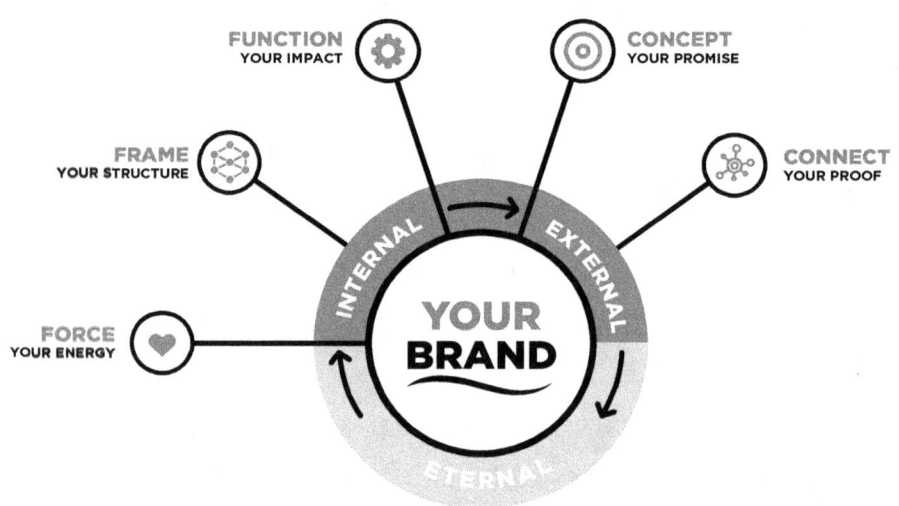

BRAND STRING THEORY

CHAPTER FOURTEEN
CONNECT TRUST

ATTENTION. TRUST. WHERE IS IT, AND WHY IS IT THERE?

Sometimes you feel like you're sitting on the wrong side in the interrogation room. It's silent except for the buzz and flicker of a single overhead light.

You're drowning in campaign calendars, SEO tricks, social posts, and email sequences trying to figure out if somebody's out there. It's all stacked in front of you in a giant evidence box and it smells like a cold case.

So many brands are addicted to "more."
More channels, more content, more something.

Do you Trust anyone who says, "Trust me?"

Remember that snake Kaa trying to hypnotize Mowgli with "Trust in Me"? The harder you push, the faster people run.

We all have moments where we're overwhelmed. We feel doubt. We second-guess. We think pushing harder is the way to go.

However:

| ***The Trust is out there.*** |

The evidence is often in plain sight. The strings connect. And you know where your customers Trust you. Where they pay attention without being asked. Where they defend you when you're not in the room.

Your FUNCTION helped you be strategic about where to show up.

Your Connect is about shifting your mindset and owning what you already know.

Trust is about focus not frequency.

You don't need to control everything everywhere. You need to own the spaces where customers pay attention.

Think about that for a second. Someone is choosing to Trust YOU, Trust YOUR BRAND. Out of every option in the universe, they're betting on you with their time, their money and their reputation.

That's not marketing. That's a privilege. And most brands treat it like a transaction.

Just another unchecked lead in the case folder.

You know those moments when GPS insists it knows where you're going, rerouting and rerouting? It's the same when your website, your customer service, and your product claims, all contradict one another.

Here's what happens when someone Trusts your brand. They become part of your story. They don't just buy your product or use your service, they become living proof that you're on track.

REALITY CHECK: Sports Lighting Company
One email changed everything. Instead of talking about lumens and specifications, they talked about the kid who makes varsity, the Friday night lights, and the path from high

school dreams to college scholarships and beyond. "Inspiring Generations." They didn't sell lighting, they sold the stage where champions are made.

Why? They knew who their customers were. Those customers weren't just buying lights. Many of them were parents, with kids competing in sports. Every installation now had a specific meaning. The company became champions for athletic excellence.

This is what your base camp can look like. Where people have already joined your team.

HubSpot owns the marketing conversation through thought leadership content marketing, educating their audience rather than chasing trends.

YETI connects with outdoor enthusiasts where they already gather, through social media and sponsored events, making their brand values visible through real user stories.

Peloton found the center of their ecosystem at their rider community app, leveraging organic interactions with belonging and competition.

Notice what happened? Each brand found their people and gave them something bigger than a product.

They gave them an identity. A purpose. A reason to exist.

They built Trust.

And Trust will stand with you when it matters.

But trust requires more than belonging. **Peloton** optimized engagement until it broke. They had the bike, the app, the hype. An obsessed community built around live classes, leaderboards, and an always-on rider ecosystem. During lockdowns, demand spiked. But the strings didn't connect: A hardware-first model, delivery misses, pricing whiplash, and highly public product-safety issues. When gyms reopened, their strategy spiraled between "equipment" and "platform."

HOKA proves that when trust is honored, it grows. Two French trail runners built "maximalist" shoes when everyone chased "minimalist." They rose through ultra-runners who became evangelists. They didn't sell rebellion. They sold relief. The downhill obsession became the story. Their Frame was defiance disguised as design. Oversized. Unapologetic. Their Function? Brick-and-mortar dominance as "the primary venue for full-price sales." With 20% year-over-year international growth, they claimed 10% of the U.S. running shoe market through 3,749 retail touchpoints, mostly wholesale partners, with only a dozen or so HOKA-owned stores. Retail sales in the U.S. jumped 26.7% while online flatlined at 0.5%. HOKA commoditizes where choice is automated, but grows in physical retail because maximalist cushioning must be experienced to be believed. To be Trusted.

Finding your people isn't the finish line. It's the starting line.

Because when they find you, they're saying "This is me." And every decision after that either keeps the promise or breaks it.

Kicking Horse doesn't just make great coffee. They make kick-ass coffee. And year after year, they deliver on their promise to kick ass.
That's not customer retention.
That's a relationship revolution.

Stop asking "How do we get more customers?"
Start asking "How do we build something worth defending?"

| *An ounce of Trust beats a ton of marketing.* |

Because when you have that, marketing becomes less necessary. They do it for you.

Trust isn't born, it's grown.

Every interaction either deepens the relationship or weakens it. Every touchpoint either proves you're worthy of their Trust or shows you're taking it for granted.

As a referee, I learned that Trust is built one call at a time. Every action has to be backed by what you say. One inconsistent moment can destroy a game and your reputation.

Your job isn't to be everywhere.

It's to be where you can be everything to someone.

Every single time.

CONNECT TRUST BRAND LAW

Trust is out there, but not everywhere.

YOUR CONNECT TRUST FIELD TEST

1. **Where do your customers already Trust you?**
   Stop looking everywhere and own the spaces where Trust already exists.

2. **What evidence are you ignoring in the data?**
   Analytics, emails, and research show you where Trust lives.

3. **Which relationships feel like transactions vs. privileges?**
   The ones that feel like privileges are where real Trust exists.

LESS IS MORE

Instead of pushing "Trust me!" you discovered where Trust lives. You stopped being overwhelmed by trying to be everywhere and started focusing where customers pay attention.

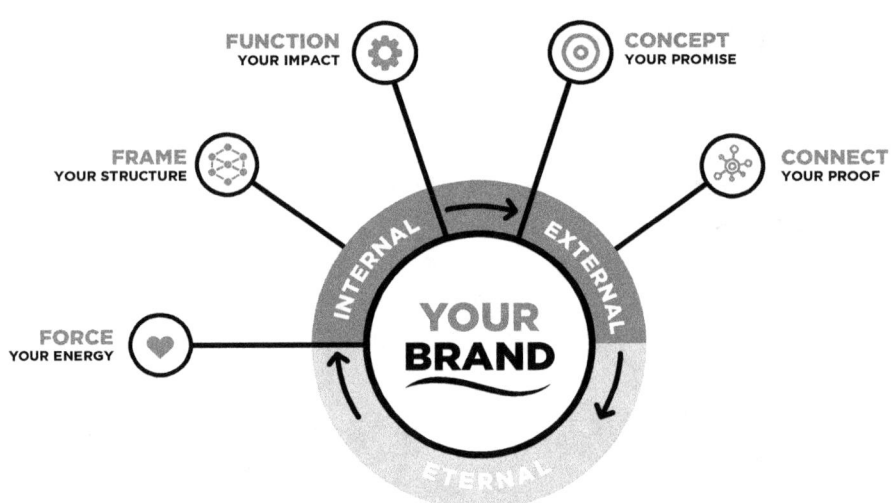

BRAND STRING THEORY

CHAPTER FIFTEEN
CONNECT JEALOUSY

WHAT BRAND SPARKS JEALOUSY (IN A GOOD WAY)?

Jealousy gets a bad rap, but it's actually insight in disguise.

It's a map to a better future.

When you see another brand and think, "Damn, I wish we'd thought of that," pay attention. That feeling isn't weakness, it's your brand instincts telling you something important about what's possible.

But here's what most people get wrong. They think "Jealousy" means "copying." It doesn't. Jealousy reveals gaps in your own brand expression that you didn't know existed or chose to ignore.
Looking at competitors isn't just about features; it's emotional.

GWI research shows that **one in five of the global consumer population are aspirational, constantly looking for brands that go beyond the transaction to create something worth talking about.**[14] That's more than a billion people.

Jealousy reveals what your brand might be holding back.

| *Jealousy is your competitive intelligence.* |

The three types of brand Jealousy:

Execution Jealousy: "I wish we'd done that first."
This is about tactics, their campaign, their design, their messaging approach, their products, their service, and their technology. It's the most common but least useful type. Example: **Netflix** killed their own DVD business to build streaming, even though DVDs were still profitable. You're

jealous of their courage to cannibalize success for growth. This Jealousy reveals where you're playing it safe when you could be playing to win.

Strategic Jealousy: "I wish we had their positioning."
You're not jealous of what they made, but where they chose to compete. They found a space you didn't see or have the courage to claim.

Example: **Liquid Death** takes absurd creative risks that could completely backfire, but they do it anyway. You're not jealous of their water product. You're jealous of their willingness to be completely ridiculous and own it.

Cultural Jealousy: "I wish we had their confidence."
This is the most valuable type. You're envious of their organizational courage. How they show up, take risks, and own their choices. Often without apologizing.

Example: **Rick Rubin,** the music producer, doesn't play instruments and has limited skills in the studio, but artists want him in the room. You might be jealous of how he knows what feels right. It's taste.

Knowing when something's ready, when to develop it further, and when to pull back.

That brings us to **AI** again. AI generates options, accelerates workflows, and spots patterns humans miss. But it can't decide when the work is done. It can copy style, but only humans know when the connections are strong enough to matter. That discernment is what AI should be really jealous of.

The confidence to trust what feels right.

I learned this running nightclubs. You see what works elsewhere and think you can just transplant it. We have all taken a "mockingbird" brand approach because we're Jealous. But tactics don't transfer, conviction does. The courage to own your approach is what matters. Always.

REALITY CHECK: Industrial Safety Equipment
They were jealous of competitors who seemed to effortlessly communicate Benefits while they got stuck explaining technical specs. But when we dug deeper, they weren't jealous of their competitors' products. They envied how competitors made safety sound urgent, not optional.
We repositioned them through a campaign that said:
"Safety isn't expensive, it's priceless."
"Safety doesn't happen by accident."
"Safety risk isn't worth it."
"Safety is an investment that returns."

Instead of battling on specs, they made safety the only thing that mattered. Safety became the reason to choose, not a bullet point to explain. Now competitors are jealous.

Jealousy Reveal
Most Jealousy reveals internal limitations, not external opportunities. You're not jealous of what they built, you're jealous of their willingness to build it despite criticism, risk, and the possibility of failure.
Here's a real example: When Apple Music entered streaming in 2015, **Spotify** didn't try to outspend them. Apple had deeper pockets and iPhone integration, but Spotify stuck to

what made them different. Apple focused on exclusives and artist deals, and banked on their ecosystem. Spotify worked everywhere. Android, web, smart speakers, your car. And they stuck to their algorithm that learned what you liked and let you share what you discovered. Today they have more than double the subscribers that Apple has globally.

Five brands that inspire productive Jealousy:

Monocle: A global media brand that blends high taste, sharp design, and cultural intelligence without feeling elitist. They make sophistication feel accessible. "Read More. Live Better." What's Jealousy-worthy? Their permission to be both intelligent and approachable.

Reformation: Built a fashion brand that started by retailoring vintage clothing and evolved into a stylish, ethical, and wildly desired brand, without compromising its tone or values. They proved you don't have to choose between profitability and principles. What's Jealousy-worthy? Their refusal to compromise their values for growth.

Bumble: Reinvented dating with a female-first approach and turned UX into a lifestyle movement. They showed how functional innovation can become cultural leadership. What's Jealousy-worthy? Their willingness to challenge social assumptions everyone else accepted.

Nando's: The South African fast food chain said no to using frozen chicken. Nando's chicken is fresh, marinated for 24 hours, and flame-grilled. Now peri-peri, a typically African hot sauce, is global because real beats convenient. What's

Jealousy-worthy? No compromise on fresh when frozen is easy.

Hello Kitty: Designer Yuko Shimizu created a character without a mouth in 1974, letting people project their own emotions onto the blank face. To "speak from the heart." What's Jealousy-worthy? The conviction that restraint creates connection when the whole industry designs for explicit expression.

What you admire in other brands reflects what you want to express in your own.

If you're jealous of:
Boldness. You're probably playing it too safe.
Clarity. You're probably overcomplicating things.
Consistency. You're probably fragmented across touchpoints.
Confidence. You're probably hedging your positioning.
Community. You're probably transactional instead of relational.
Permission. You're probably asking for approval instead of taking action.

| *Jealousy is diagnostic. It shows you where your brand could grow.* |

Smart brands give themselves permission to:
Say no to opportunities that don't fit.
Charge what they're worth.
Stand for something specific.
Risk alienating people who aren't their customers anyway.
Be remarkable instead of safe.

Make decisions based on their principles, not their fears. You're not jealous of their success. You're jealous of their certainty.

Give yourself permission to turn jealousy into action.

Build something they'd search for if it went missing.

CONNECT JEALOUSY **BRAND LAW**

Use **Jealousy** as competitive and strategic intelligence.

YOUR CONNECT JEALOUSY FIELD TEST

1. **What brands make you think, "I wish we'd thought of that?"**
   Identify what you actually admire to understand your own aspirations.

2. **What specific elements of their success could you adapt to your brand?**
   Study the structure and principles, not just the style.

3. **What would you attempt if you had their level of confidence?**
   Use their boldness to examine your own self-imposed limitations.

LESS IS MORE

You stopped seeing other brands as threats and started using them as teachers. You eliminated the fear of being influenced and started being intentional about what influences you.

EXTERNAL CONVERT

Not everyone says yes.
You build it.
Your CONVERT.
To make commitment feel natural.

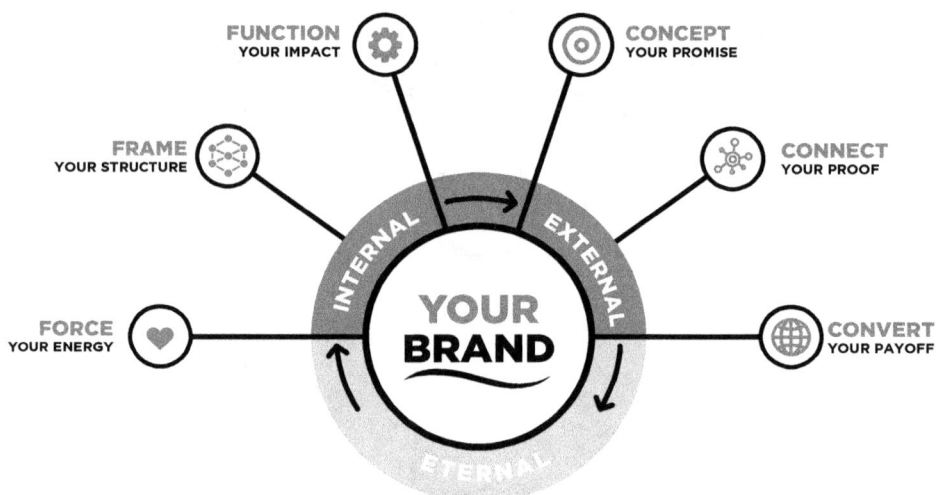

BRAND STRING THEORY

CHAPTER SIXTEEN
CONVERT COMMITMENT

THERE'S COMMITMENT. WHAT HAPPENS NEXT?

Calling all call-to-actions.

Do we love buttons? Or do we hate buttons?

And we've clicked buttons that have made our day, week, month and year. And clicked ones that have taken us to meet the dark rabbit Frank.

It can be frustrating. Even more so when you're the one needing them to convert.

I have a test for your button, your text link, your call-to-action (CTA, as it's commonly referred to).

First, consider this: Your CTA is often the first thing people read.

Why? Because you've been told to make it stand out! Use contrasting colors, place it above the fold, bottom right, and so forth. So yes, it's often read even before the headline. And that makes it even more critical.

Back to my test.

The COMMITMENT ISOLATION TEST™

Look at your layout or design. You may have six elements on your homepage hero section, landing page, or ad.

Let's say it's a website.

You may have the following components: eyebrow copy, a

headline, a content section, an image, and social proof.

Keep your button visible and remove everything else except one component.

Test each of these:
1. Eyebrow copy + CTA
2. Headline + CTA
3. Content copy + CTA
4. Social proof + CTA
5. Image + CTA

Basic website layout:

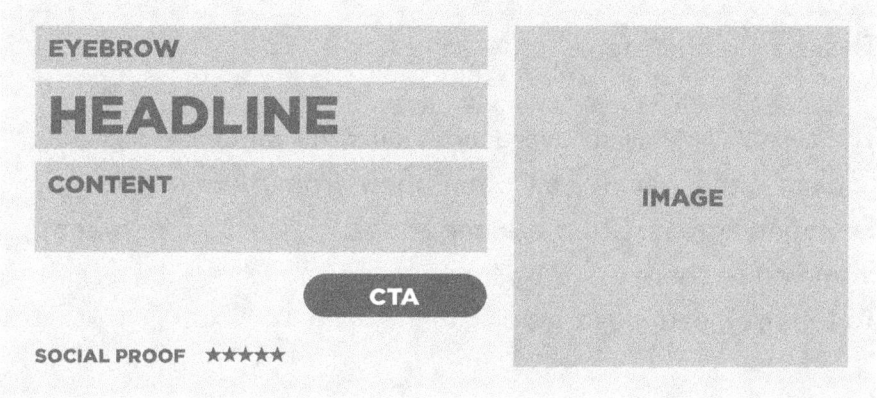

Your CTA should make sense with every single component, independent of the other components.

Does it tell people exactly what to do?
And more importantly, what they'll get?

For all of the above to work, your CTA should also work as a standalone. So, when you remove everything except your CTA, where does it leave the user?

"Learn More?" Okay.
"Contact Us?" Why?.
"Get Started?" With what?

If your CTA can't stand on its own, it's weak. If it only works in full context, it means that when someone scans your page (which is how most people read), your CTA has lost its power.

Strong CTAs pass **The Commitment Isolation Test™**:
They work with every element independently.
They work alone.
They show two-way commitment.
They promise an outcome, not a process.

This is a Commitment.

The term "CTA" is so overused it's lost its value for me. Look at it this way: It's a Commitment from them to you. Everyone agrees. But more importantly, it's a Commitment from you to them.
To the user, your customer.

| **Commitment works both ways.** |

If you know what to do, then they know what to do.

REALITY CHECK: Software Development Company
Their website talked about "Top-Rated Development Partner." "Hire Top Developers." "Proven Talent." "Your satisfaction is 100% guaranteed!" And the Commitment? "Get a Free Strategy Call." Does it make sense because most calls in their industry cost something?

There was no Commitment being delivered to potential clients.

I led with "79.2% of Websites Run on PHP." (I didn't know that, and my sports software runs on PHP, the programming language.)

I developed the concept of PRECISION PHP™. Their proprietary methodology, which positioned them as established experts.
The Commitment was "Let's Talk PHP Business."

If a buyer is still undecided, then there's a DISCOVERY button, that delivers a Free PRECISION PHP™ Guide PDF. Nurturing content before they're ready to commit.

The result is that they now own their Commitment to customers as experts that will deliver.

According to multiple studies, **personalized CTAs perform 202% better than basic ones.**[15] People don't need persuasion; they need precision. One clear action, clearly stated, and backed by your Commitment to the customer, makes the difference.

What makes a Commitment work?

Specific over generic:

Don't tell them what you do. Tell them what they're protecting.
Don't offer a service. Offer a shield.

Your Commitment connects to your FORCE, FRAME and FUNCTION. When it does, it's not just an instruction... it's a promise that only you can make.

| ***Think outcome over process. Authority over accessibility.*** |

Look at Commitments that get this right:
"Let's Talk PHP Business" positions them as business strategists, not just developers. That's authority, not accessibility.

MasterClass: "Contact Us" would be accessibility. "Learn from the Best" is authority. You're not reaching out, you're accessing mastery.

Duolingo: "Start Learning" would be process. "Become Fluent" is outcome. You're not doing lessons, you're transforming into someone who speaks another language.

Notice how each Commitment reflects what the company stands for? That's no accident.

Process tells them what to do. Outcome tells them what they'll become. Accessibility makes you available. Authority makes you essential.

Your Commitment isn't about getting clicks. It's about giving clear direction to people who are ready to move forward.

It's a Commitment that you need to keep.

CONVERT COMMITMENT BRAND LAW

Commitment works both ways.

YOUR CONVERT COMMITMENT FIELD TEST

1. **Do you pass the Commitment Isolation Test™?**
   If your Commitment can't stand with each element, or alone, it's broken.

2. **Is it a two-way promise or just asking for clicks?**
   Real Commitments work both ways: From them to you, and you to them.

3. **Does it show outcome over process, authority over accessibility?**
   "Contact Us" is accessibility. "Talk to the Experts" is authority. "Start Learning" is process. "Become Fluent" is outcome.

LESS IS MORE

You stopped asking for clicks and started making promises you can deliver on. Your Commitment now builds Trust instead of just traffic.

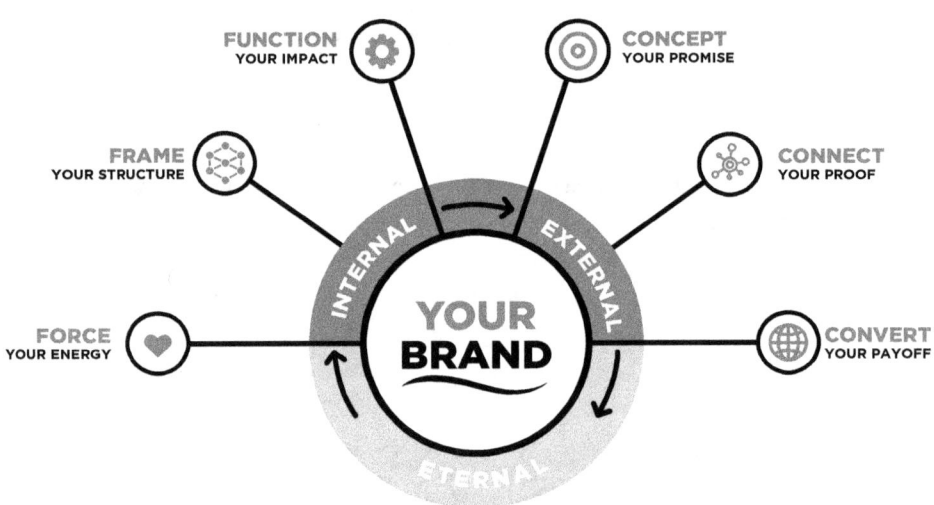

CHAPTER SEVENTEEN
CONVERT EXCUSE

WHY THE EXCUSE, THE HESITATION?

The Baymard Institute found that **70.19% of online carts are abandoned**,[16] most often due to unclear next steps, hidden costs, or poor mobile user experience (UX). Even tiny blockers kill conversion momentum.

You think it's price. It's usually process.
You think it's competition. It's usually confusion.
You think it's trust. It's usually unintentional friction.

The biggest conversion killer isn't objection. It's hesitation.

| *When people hesitate, they're mostly gone. Mostly.* |

I learned this as a DJ playing 10-hour sets. The moment the energy drops, people head to the bar... or worse, they head home. You don't get them back by playing the same song louder. You get them back by removing whatever caused the energy drop in the first place.

Don't blame the DJ. Fix the floor.
Conversion works the same way: Find the energy drop. Fix it.

REALITY CHECK: Architectural Design Manufacturer
They wanted to expand their reach with architects but faced a credibility obstacle. Their Commitment had to be preceded by discovery, "Register for Webinar," with a supporting line: "Systems for Technical Spaces." The first obstacle wasn't lack of interest, architects needed proof of expertise upfront. The webinar provided attendees continuing education while positioning the manufacturer as experts across the industry. They promoted themselves through LinkedIn and industry channels to establish authority.

And there was a second obstacle: Their webinar registration form asked for company size, project types, budget, timeline, and technical specifications. By question three, architects felt like they were in a deposition. We stripped it down to three fields: Name, email, and "What type of spaces do you design?" Webinar registration rates jumped.

Same company, same expertise, different approach that eliminated both the "prove it" barrier and the "interrogation" barrier while building their expert reputation.

That's the pattern. Find the hesitation, remove the negative friction. Here's how others do it:

Loom: Their Commitment is literally "Record a Video." Their Commitment is action: Hit record fast on a free plan. No Excuses.
Typeform: They make complex sign-ups feel like conversations, not interrogations. Information gathering becomes engagement.
Chewy: Reordering pet food is one-click because they know when you'll run out. Timing obstacles eliminated.

What they're really thinking...
Your prospects are in three states simultaneously: In Market, In Flux, or In Doubt.

In Market
They're actively looking. Something pushed them to search. But what are they really worried about? Price? Quality? Integration? Results? Address the worry, don't avoid it.

Calendly: Proves you're not alone in switching. 20 million people already made this exact decision. You're not the guinea pig, you're joining the majority.

In Flux

They want to solve this, but when? Today? Next quarter? They need to know what happens if they wait vs. what happens if they move now. Give them a reason to act, not just information to consider.

Slack: Removes the timing pressure completely. No contracts, no credit cards, no IT approval needed. You can test it with your team this afternoon and kill it tomorrow if it doesn't work.

In Doubt

They're either not really interested, not ready, or they've been burned before. Everyone has. What do they need to believe that you're different? Not everything you want to tell them. Just what they need to feel confident. The smallest possible Commitment wins. Don't ask for marriage on the first date. What's the lowest-risk way to start?

Shopify: "Get 3 days free, then 3 months for $1/month." They give you three days to test everything, then three months to build your business for basically nothing. By month four, you're either making money or you're out three dollars. (Plus tax).

That's the difference between understanding their state and honestly addressing it.

The B2B Excuse

Reality
Your biggest competitor isn't another company. It's the status quo. It's "We'll think about it." It's "Maybe next quarter." Because if they have to work to give you money, they'll find someone who makes it easier.

Mobile
Most B2B buyers use mobile during their research, and mobile now influences over 40% of revenue in leading companies, but most B2B sites still assume desktop decisions.

Politics
Decision-making politics. Your buyer needs to sell you internally. Give them the tools that make them the expert in the room.

Costs
Not your price, but their cost of integration. What does implementation actually look like? How long until they see results? Answer these before they ask.

Vendors
They may be locked in a contract already. Give them ammunition to switch when it expires, or tools to bring you in alongside existing vendors.

But here's what most brands miss about hesitation. It's not just killing your conversions; it's also killing your progress.

Wrong action beats perfect inaction.

You'll learn more in one week of real customer feedback than six months of internal meetings about your tagline.

Every day you hesitate, someone else is building momentum.

You can edit something until the world runs out of ink. Test while others debate fonts.

The market teaches faster than your meetings. Take action and avoid terminal analysis.

The Attack
Find the energy drop. Fix the floor. Don't add more persuasion. Remove unnecessary friction. The goal isn't to convince harder, it's to make deciding easier.

Stop fighting for attention.

Start removing hesitation.

CONVERT EXCUSE BRAND LAW

Remove the **Excuse.** Earn the Commitment.

YOUR CONVERT EXCUSE FIELD TEST

1. **What's making them hesitate right now?**
   Map the actual problem points, not the assumed ones.

2. **What's the smallest possible Commitment you can ask for?**
   This is not a deposition.

3. **What do they need to believe to move forward?**
   Address their worry, don't avoid it.

LESS IS MORE

You stopped trying to convince and started making it easier for them to decide. Bad friction and persuasion eliminated. Your opportunity to CONVERT is now ready.

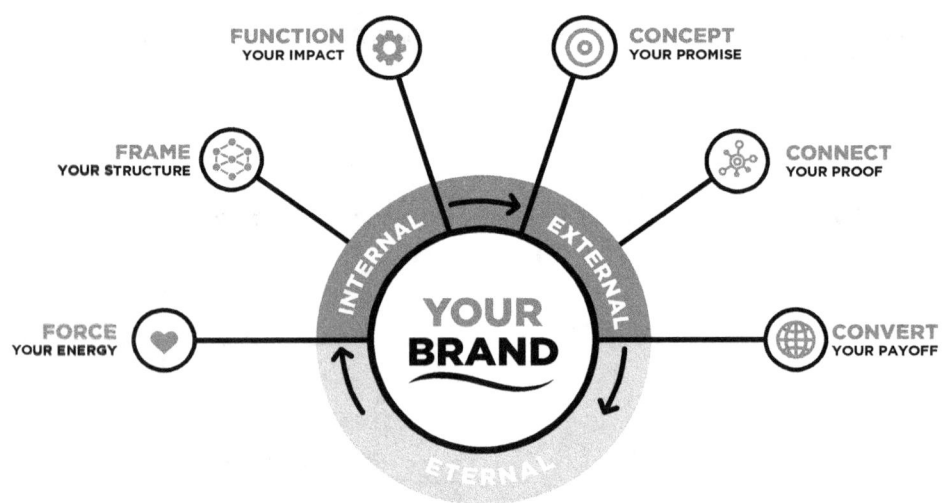

BRAND STRING THEORY

CHAPTER EIGHTEEN
CONVERT FUTURE

WHEN THEY SAY YES TO THEIR FUTURE, WHAT CHANGES?

When someone makes a Commitment to you, what changes in their world?

That's not a marketing question. That's a vision question.

| Don't sell clicks. Sell the change. |

Running nightclubs, the goal wasn't getting people through the door; it was creating an experience they'd talk about for the rest of their lives. The entrance fee was just access. The real value was transformation. For hours, you weren't stuck in your cubicle mindset or your daily grind. You were part of something bigger.

Your brand works like that. The Commitment is just access. The transformation is what they really bought.

REALITY CHECK: Marketing Platform
Their Commitment was "Sign Up Free." A 14-day trial. "Because everyone can learn a marketing platform in 14 days," said no one. So, you wonder, what's the vision? What changes when someone commits to their platform? Their vision should be: "Build Your Business. 30 Days Free." Small businesses don't sign up for email marketing. They commit to growing their customer relationships, increasing sales, and building something sustainable.

The Commitment is about the platform. The vision is about their Future. When the two align, the 30 days becomes about building something meaningful.

And, **30-day trials convert 273% more than 14-day trials** according to Techround.[17] It's not about more clicks, it's about more traction in the right direction.

But here's what brands miss: Every Commitment should ladder up to something bigger. Not just for you. For them.

The Change Ladder
- **24 hours:** What feels different tomorrow?
- **30 days:** What gets easier or starts working?
- **12 months:** What becomes possible?

If you can't answer that for them, you're just optimizing for traffic, not transformation.

Look at brands that connect Commitment to vision:

LinkedIn: Profile today. Bigger network tomorrow. Career change down the line.
Hims & Hers: Fix the problem today. Build confidence tomorrow. Feel like yourself again.
Kit (formerly ConvertKit): Sign up, build an audience, eventually buy your own freedom.

Every Commitment should make the next step easier because the hard work shouldn't start after they commit.

The Commitment Reality

Clicks are stats.
Commitment is compound interest.
Don't let every yes be just another transaction.

Attach every Commitment to the transformation it enables.

If people don't see what they become tomorrow, next month, a year from now, they're just passing through.

Sell the change that's needed for the Future.

Because people don't search for transactions. They search for transformations that matter.

CONVERT FUTURE BRAND LAW

For every Commitment, sell the change and the **Future**.

YOUR CONVERT FUTURE FIELD TEST

1. **What's different for them tomorrow after they say yes?**
   If you can't name it, they can't feel it.

2. **What happens if they stick with you for longer?**
   The growth must be obvious.

3. **Does each Commitment make the next one easier?**
   Build momentum through relationship progression.

LESS IS MORE

You stopped optimizing for transactions
and started designing for the Future.
Conversions now build relationships worth keeping.
Your growth just became predictable instead of random.

BRAND STRING THEORY™

EXTERNAL CASE STUDY
DYSON

Dyson started with rage. Sick of vacuum bags and loss of suction. 5,127 prototypes later, they engineered the answer. Cyclone technology that worked. That obsession became their FORCE: Engineering that reinvents how we live.

That engineering went into hair dryers that don't fry, air purifiers that show what you're breathing, and bladeless fans. Each category with the same FRAME: It works or doesn't ship. And a genius move? Stealing Apple's retail playbook. 450 demo stores worldwide where you experience before buying. Touch the $600 hair dryer. While competitors hid in big-box stores, Dyson built engineering temples.

With 27% US market share, they proved that perfect products beat perfect service. Their CONVERT fails. One-way promises, nightmare support, impossible repairs. People still buy. Imagine if they fixed aftercare.

What works. The Dyson Brand String Theory Analysis.

DYSON INTERNAL

	FORCE	
WORTH (THEN)	✓	Vacuums use bags, lose power and suction. Fix it.
WORTH (NOW)	✓	Appliances deserve the best engineering.
CHANGE	✓	Fighting everyday inferior products.
DISAPPEARED	✓	The world's trusted partner in new appliance tech.
	FRAME	
BELIEF	✓	Works or doesn't ship. 5,127 prototypes.
PRINCIPLE	✓	Engineering first, no compromise.
FORGED	✓	It just works better.
	FUNCTION	
POSITION	✓	Premium engineering showcases.
WORKS	✓	Creates loyal customers, behavior changes.
FRICTION	✗	Impossible repairs and no support.

DYSON EXTERNAL

	CONCEPT	
HOOK	✓	Superior engineering that works.
SENTENCE	✓	Engineering that solves real problems.
TODAY	✓	Constantly evolving: Air, hair, climate, + more.
	CONNECT	
BENEFITS	✓	Educational storytelling. Teach, not sell.
TRUST	✓	Digital, social, retail demo stores.
JEALOUSY	✓	Copied Apple's retail playbook.
	CONVERT	
COMMITMENT	✗	One-way sale, no promise back.
EXCUSE	✗	High price.
FUTURE	✓	Transformation to high end, high tech.

WORKING BRAND LAWS
UNDER PRESSURE

Brand success through the Brand String Theory lens.

STANLEY:
A Century of Brand Laws Tested in One Viral Moment

Stanley made thermoses for a century. Blue collar. Utilitarian. Besides keeping contents piping hot or icy cold, their external hook was "It Will Not Break."

In 2016, they launched the Adventure Quencher. Another industrial tool. A 40oz tumbler for jobsites. Nobody cared. It bombed. Retailers dumped it. By 2019, Stanley had all but given up. The Quencher was silently disappearing.

Then The Buy Guide resurrected it. This shopping blog convinced influencer Emily Maynard Johnson to post about the forgotten tumbler. One Instagram post changed everything.

Stanley saw the numbers. The Buy Guide had sold 5,000 units fast. Comments flooded in. Consumers wanted colors. They wanted it as an accessory, not a tool. Stanley bet everything on transformation. Hired Terence Reilly from Crocs. New colors dropped. Limited editions. Scarcity releases. Social media exploded.

Same engineering. Revolutionary positioning. Stanley's century-old foundation could support complete lifestyle transformation. The Quencher exploded Stanley from $70M to $750M.

STANLEY INTERNAL

	FORCE	
WORTH	✓	Everyone deserves status and respect.
CHANGE	✓	Premium, durable gear is for everyone.
DISAPPEARED	✓	Industrial tools as status symbols would be gone.

	FRAME	
BELIEF	✓	If it breaks, we didn't engineer it.
PRINCIPLE	✓	Build once, buy once, lasts forever.
FORGED	✓	"Unbreakable" as the Forged identity.

	FUNCTION	
POSITION	✓	Lifestyle durability.
WORKS	✓	Creates trust and belonging.
FRICTION	✓	Premium pricing justified by lifetime value.

STANLEY EXTERNAL (BEFORE/AFTER)

	CONCEPT	
HOOK	Durability you can trust.	Durability you can trust.
SENTENCE	"It Will Not Break."	Built for life, built for lifestyle.
TODAY	Industrial utility.	Lifestyle status with industrial backbone.

	CONNECT	
BENEFITS	Survives jobsites.	Built to survive, carried for status.
TRUST	On the worksite.	On the worksite and in social culture.
JEALOUSY	Confined to industrial utility.	Utility without boundaries.

	CONVERT	
COMMITMENT	Buy once, keep forever.	A purchase with a lifetime of trust.
EXCUSE	Premium justified by durability.	Premium justified by durability.
FUTURE	Always a work tool.	Built for life, built for style.

QUICK CASE STUDY: NETFLIX | *THE PASSWORD CRACKDOWN*

Netflix built their business eliminating intermediaries. They took on Blockbuster, scheduled TV, and cable gatekeepers, delivering customer access to content.

By 2019, password sharing had created a new barrier... Account owners sharing access with others. Netflix had to choose: Ignore their founding principle or enforce household boundaries.
They stayed true to their foundation. Every household deserves direct access, not borrowed access.

What stood firm for NETFLIX was their FRAME.
BELIEF: Customer meets content (eliminate all barriers).
PRINCIPLE: One subscription. Full access.
FORGED: Control your entertainment schedule.

So when they tackled the issue, their Belief (their yes/no machine), and their Principle were there for their EXTERNAL campaign.

CONCEPT: "Your Netflix account is for you and the people you live with, your household."
CONNECT: Clear household boundaries protect your viewing control.
CONVERT: Simple options, transfer profiles, buy extra member, start your own account.

RESULT: 19M new subscribers. Their internal engine drove external success by staying consistent across 25 years.

QUICK CASE STUDY: DUOLINGO | *THE CHAOTIC OWL*

Duolingo was founded to break elitism in education. Language learning had been locked behind schools, tuition, and expensive software, like Rosetta Stone. They delivered free access to anyone with a phone.

By 2020, the problem wasn't access, it was attention. Millions downloaded the app but dropped off quickly. Then the streak reminders became memes. Users turned the owl into a chaotic, obsessive character. Duolingo had to choose to make the meme theirs.

They stayed true to their foundation: Education should be free, fun, and rewarding. DUOLINGO's FRAME did the work.
BELIEF: Education is a right, not a privilege.
PRINCIPLE: Learning feels like play.
FORGED: Don't study, play and learn every day.

So when the memes became their identity, their yes/no machine and their principle were there for their EXTERNAL campaign.
CONCEPT: The streak is the game. Keep it alive.
CONNECT: The owl became the cultural magnet. Chaotic, funny, unforgettable.
CONVERT: Users didn't just learn; they showed up daily, obsessed with streaks, turning free play into paid subscriptions.

RESULT: Duolingo doubled daily active users and became the most downloaded education app in the world. Their internal engine drove external success by staying consistent: Learning as play, amplified by culture.

BRAND STRING THEORY

What you're really here to do.
ETERNAL

**RECKONING
RECOGNIZE
RELEASE**

BRAND STRING THEORY

ETERNAL RECKONING

We often settle for "good enough."
You build it.
Your RECKONING.
Who you are when it matters most.

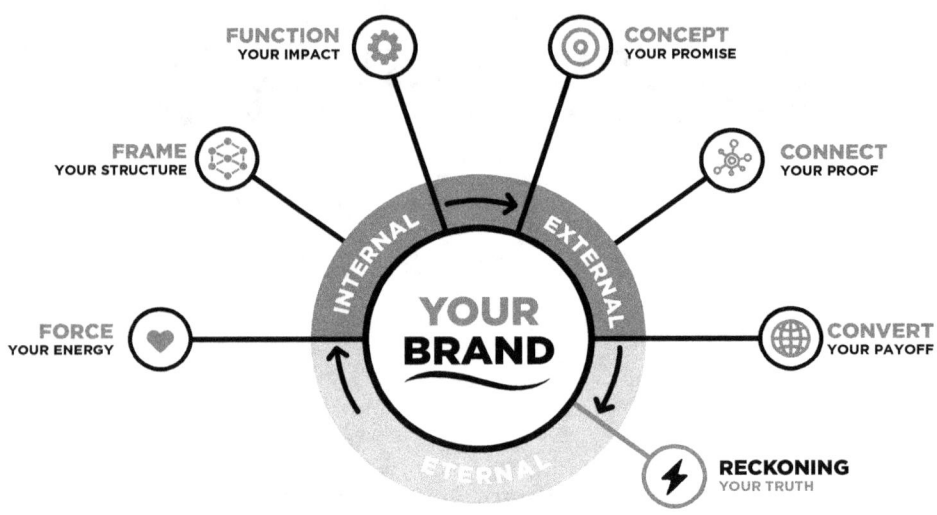

BRAND STRING THEORY

CHAPTER NINETEEN
RECKONING TRUTH

DO YOU KNOW THE TRUTH, BUT HAVEN'T TOLD ANYONE?

You've built your FORCE, designed your FRAME, defined your FUNCTION, clarified your CONCEPT, perfected your CONNECT, and optimized your CONVERT.

But, do you trust yourself to always tell the truth?

You know what you want to be known for. You've always known. But you've been too scared, too professional, too responsible to say it.

"Good enough" gets you nowhere.

Your secret brand ambition isn't to have more ambition. It's not a nice-to-have. It's not a someday dream. It's the only thing standing between building a forgettable business and one that matters. Every legendary brand started by saying what others were afraid to admit.

A 2025 issue of ScienceDirect published that **brands with bold public stances (even polarizing ones) gained 29% more organic traffic and 2x higher brand recall.**[18] Playing it safe can be "good enough," but it's risky.

So, just between us: Say it! And say it out loud.

| *Your secret ambition is your strategy.* |

Are you lying for attention?
I've worked with so many brands, and they all have the same disease. You do all the work, and then you second guess yourself, your team, and you're back to where you started. It's terminal safety syndrome.

The symptoms? You doubt yourself and return to generic messaging. Safe positioning that offends and excites no one. Corporate jargon that says nothing. And the bottleneck is back. The prognosis is forgettable.

And it's dangerous. You can fall into the trap of saying something that is not fundamentally true. If you don't have your INTERNAL FORCE, FRAME, and FUNCTION consistently aligned, with solid beliefs and principles, to deliver your EXTERNAL CONCEPT, CONNECT and CONVERT, then the face that you show the world is not the Truth.

You know what you really want to be known for, but you're back to dressing it up in corporate speak until it sounds like everyone else. You settle for "good enough" when you could own something.

The accounting firm that wants to be "the CFO that makes other CFOs obsolete" but calls themselves "trusted business advisors."

You're back in the crowd that are playing that way. The many that have settled for good enough.

The Committee Problem
Brands operate like a four-person committee making every decision. The CEO wants to be bold. The marketing director wants to be safe. The sales team wants to please everyone. Legal wants you to say nothing.
Result? "Good enough" systems and messaging that nobody remembers. You know what nobody in that committee did? The work you just did.

The best brands kill the committee and say what they mean.

The Ambition Categories
Category 1: Industry Annihilation
You don't want to compete. You want to make the entire industry obsolete. **Uber:** "We're not improving taxis. We're eliminating them."

Category 2: Cultural Revolution
You want to change how people think, not just what they buy. **Chobani:** "We're not making yogurt. We're proving business can be a force for good."

Category 3: Human Transformation
You want to change who your customers become, not just what they have. **CrossFit:** "We don't sell gym memberships. We forge warriors."

REALITY CHECK: Benetton - Truth without foundation
In the 90s, they didn't whisper about "heritage" or "Italian quality." They threw their sweaters into the background and shoved hard truths into the spotlight. "United Colors" was AIDS patients in hospital beds. Death row inmates staring back at you. Newborn babies fresh from the womb. Racism, war, inequality, photographed, printed, and plastered across billboards.

Benetton showed their RECKONING but never built the system to hold it all together. They didn't have a yes/no machine. They said yes to everything shocking. Not principle. Sensation. Not clarity. Chaos. Not a filter. A free-for-all. That's why the RECKONING burned hot and burned out.

So, what do you really sell?

The permission you don't need:
Nobody's going to give you permission to be different.
Your board won't vote on it.
Your customers won't request it.
Your industry won't encourage it.
Your parents won't understand it.

Permission comes from deciding that your brand's impact matters more than playing it safe.

It's your RECKONING.
What would you build if you had three years left?
What in your industry frustrates you to the end of time?
What would you say if no one could stop you?
Not what sounds good in a mission statement.
What keeps you up at night with excitement?

Here's an example.
Financial Planner says: "We offer personalized planning services."
What they really want to say: "We build wealth that lasts generations."
What they should say: "We don't manage money. We build family empires."
The first version sounds like everyone else. The second sounds like someone you'd actually want to work with. But the third makes competitors irrelevant.

Glossier: Emily Weiss had a secret: Beauty marketing was top-down. Glossier built it bottom-up. Their RECKONING: "What if beauty marketing reflected how women actually think?" They created conversational marketing that felt like advice from friends, not beauty counter pressure. Revenue: Zero to $200M in 10 years by making beauty feel approachable.

RECKONING Examples:
Dyson: "We fix what everyone else accepts as standard."
Stanley (after the Quencher success): "We prove that industrial toughness belongs beyond the job site."
Slack: Work communication doesn't need email, real-time channels work better.

Here's what happens.
If you keep playing it safe, you sound exactly like your competitors, compete on price, and nobody remembers you exist.

If you own what you believe, wrong customers leave, and right customers join. Price becomes irrelevant, and the competition gets nervous.

It's natural.

As Anna says, "There is so much beauty in what is natural. If you don't take advantage of that, you really miss out." The spaces she designs and builds feel inevitable. Following the Bauhaus maxim: "Truth to materials as a central principle," her buildings feel exactly the way they should. This is about selecting and using materials to their natural potential.

So you have to ask yourself: What's natural about how you work that you're not talking about? What's obvious to you that's revolutionary to others? Your brand's integrity.

When you've built your INTERNAL engine and your EXTERNAL execution delivers, ETERNAL is where you step into what you're really here to do.

Your customers want you to be honest about what you do. They're also bored by "good enough."

Stop doubting the work you've done to get here.

Stop asking for permission.

Be honest. That's your Truth.

RECKONING TRUTH BRAND LAW

Don't lie for attention. Trust yourself. Tell the **Truth**.

YOUR RECKONING TRUTH FIELD TEST

1. **If time was running out, what would you stop pretending to care about?**
   Tear up your to-do list. What's the one thing that would matter if the clock was ticking?

2. **What untruth does your industry protect, and why are you done playing along?**
   Anger isn't a flaw; it's direction. Burn the script!

3. **What Truth have you never said out loud because it scares you?**
   That's what's worth building a brand around.

LESS IS MORE

You backed yourself. You eliminated the fear of judgment and built something worth remembering.
Your brand became intentional, not accidental.

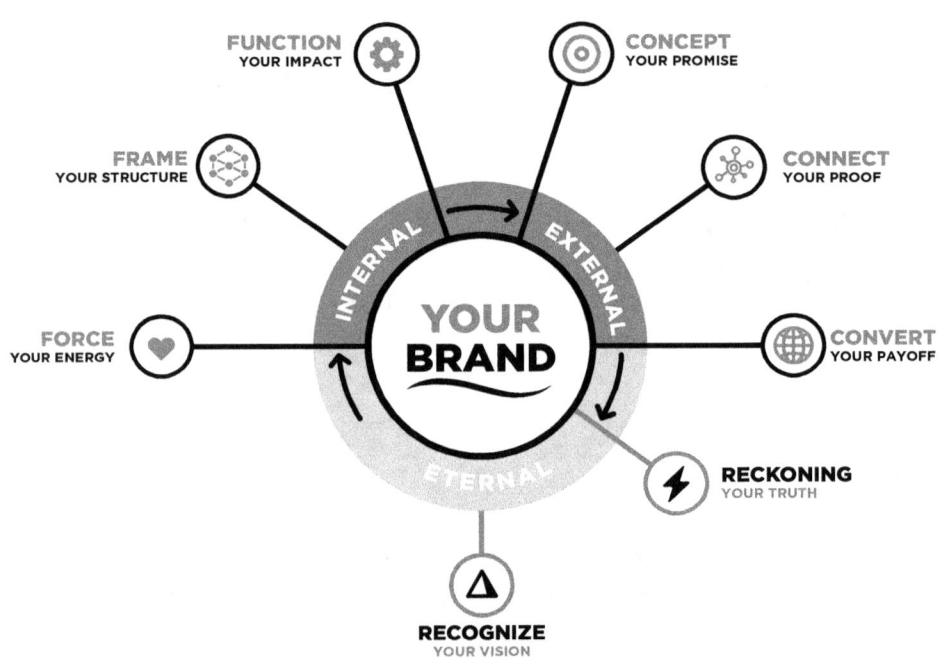

BRAND STRING THEORY

CHAPTER TWENTY
RECOGNIZE VISION

YOUR BRAND HAS VISION. WHAT DO YOU SEE?

Vision is the automatic perspective that proves your brand's INTERNAL engine is fully aligned. That you trust what you've built. It's what your brand sees when it's no longer trying to look.

Princeton psychologists researched and published in Psychological Science that **people can form impressions about personality and trust in less than 100 milliseconds.**[19]

With your INTERNAL aligned, you immediately see clarity. Other brands stumble into rooms making incorrect assumptions. You see what matters.

| *First impressions can last a lifetime.* |

Your perspective is now predictable.

The Evidence Board
Picture this: Everything on the evidence board connects.

A brand built to fix broken systems sees inefficiency everywhere.
A brand forged by principles sees who's isolated.
A brand positioned in the right place sees what's being accepted.

What your brand sees first is always a reflection of its FORCE, FRAME and FUNCTION.

Your Vision is your INTERNAL engine in action. The pattern recognition that makes opportunities obvious to you while everyone else stays blind.

REALITY CHECK: Bellator Fighting Championships
When I asked them what their brand would see on the evidence board, the answer was immediate:
"The person who thinks they're the toughest in the room. And the exact moment we'd be tougher."

That wasn't marketing speak. That was Vision.

They didn't need a brand workshop to figure that out. Their FORCE (combat sports lack respect and legitimacy) plus their FRAME (dominance through discipline) plus their FUNCTION (where fighters prove themselves) created inevitable perspective.

They couldn't look at their industry and not see hierarchy and conquest. The evidence board showed them what everyone else had missed: MMA needed a legitimate challenger to UFC's dominance.

The logo I developed was a battle-hardened Roman centurion. A face hidden in shadows. Every visual element flowed from that core perspective. They didn't see networking opportunities. They saw conquest opportunities.

Within five years they became a serious competitor to UFC and were eventually acquired for millions.

In beer, safe is everywhere. **BrewDog** studied the evidence board of an industry under siege. Equity for Punks, beers in stuffed squirrels, and an "anti-corporate" stance that made "big beer" look ancient. Their execution wasn't hops. It was hostility.

They didn't choose to see corporate beer as the enemy. Their FORCE, that craft beer had been domesticated, made it impossible for them to see anything else.

As a referee, I learned that under pressure, your INTERNAL engine is critical to surviving the final minutes of a game. My Vision wasn't about making one perfect call; it was creating an environment where both teams trusted the game would be fair. When you have that Vision, you don't get caught up in the moment. You see it all. You let the teams decide the outcome because your complete foundation has already been built for them to compete.

Most brands see what they think they should:
Safe networking.
Ways to fit in.
Permission to explain.
Chances to avoid controversy.

That's brand delusion.

Multiple Visions depending on the platform?

LinkedIn professional, Instagram casual, proposals corporate.

That's blurred Vision.

Your Vision isn't about politeness. It's about perspective.

| **Your brand should see the same Vision everywhere.** |

The Five Types of Vision

The Conqueror: Markets to influence, not enter. **Amazon** doesn't see retail spaces, they see territories to absorb.

The Connector: Islands that need bridges, people who need each other. **Zoom** doesn't see video calls, they see separated humans who belong together.

The Authority: Respect that's already theirs, just unrecognized. **Goldman Sachs** doesn't see pitching opportunities, they see people who need their guidance.

The Rebel: Rules begging to be broken, permission waiting to be seized. **Banksy** doesn't see walls, they see blank canvases everywhere.

The Revolutionary: Systems ready for complete reconstruction. **TikTok** doesn't see social media, they see human attention patterns ready for rewiring.

Brands that see every string:

Red Bull: Sees the extraordinary. Every interaction is a chance to make something impossible feel inevitable.

Fenty Beauty: Sees beauty standards that exclude instead of include. Every product is a chance to redefine what's possible.

A24 Films: Sees stories everyone else thinks won't sell. Every film is proof that weird works.

The String Test
Let's use **Allbirds**.

String 1 – Website visit: What does the brand see in their visitor's real problem? *Comfortable shoes shouldn't poison the planet.*

String 2 – Sales conversation: What does the brand see in their situation that others don't? *Sustainable doesn't mean sacrifice. Natural performs better.*

String 3 – Social media: What does the brand see in culture that needs addressing? *Fashion dumps on the planet. Shoes don't have to.*

String 4 – Crisis: What does the brand see in the problem that reveals the solution? *Climate anxiety creates demand. Transparency beats greenwashing.*

Same anchor everywhere:
Synthetic is the enemy, natural is the answer.

RECOGNIZE Examples

Your Vision becomes automatic when your internal engine is complete.

Dyson: Sees engineering problems hiding in plain sight, in every product category.

Stanley: Sees "unbreakable" working everywhere, not just on jobsites.

Slack: sees email chaos (threads, cc's, lost context) in every workplace communication.

But you don't really know your Vision until you pressure test it.

The Pressure Test
Crisis hits. Competitors attack. Customers rage.
Your brand sees what it can't help but see.

Bellator saw conquest. **BrewDog** saw betrayal. I saw fairness on the rugby field.

Your FORCE, FRAME, and FUNCTION make your Vision deliberate.

You see it all. Your Vision has become automatic.

You can't turn it off. You can't fake it.

You're not doing branding anymore.

You are your brand.

RECOGNIZE VISION BRAND LAW

Vision is what your brand automatically sees.

YOUR RECOGNIZE VISION FIELD TEST

1. **What does your brand see first in any situation?**
   Define the pattern, problem, or opportunity you spot immediately before analysis, before research, before anyone else does.

2. **What does your brand see that competitors overlook?**
   Identify what your Vision filter catches that others miss, accept, or normalize.

3. **Does your brand see the same thing everywhere?**
   Test consistency: Website, sales conversations, social media, crisis moments. Same perspective every time?

LESS IS MORE

You stopped questioning your approach and started trusting your perspective. Your Vision became automatic, your advantage became strategic.

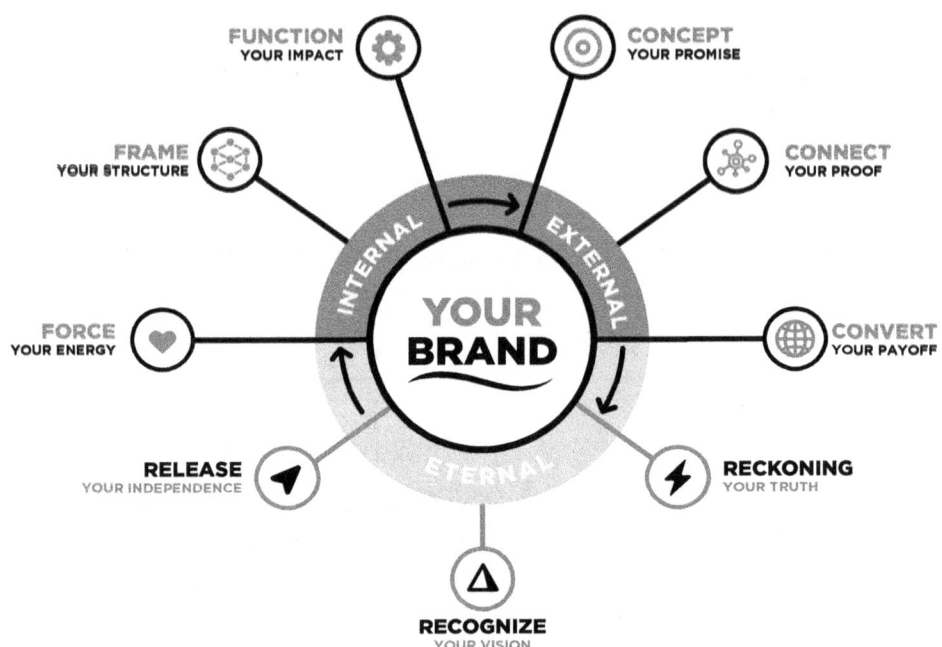

BRAND STRING THEORY

CHAPTER TWENTY-ONE
RELEASE INDEPENDENCE

YOUR INDUSTRY INDEPENDENCE IN SECONDS. ARE YOU READY?

Everything you've built leads to this moment.

You've found your FORCE.
You've built your FRAME.
You've defined your FUNCTION.
You've clarified your CONCEPT.
You've designed your CONNECT.
You've optimized your CONVERT.

You've done the work.
Now RELEASE your Independence in seconds.

| *This isn't an elevator pitch. It's a declaration of Independence.* |

When your Brand String Theory is connected, Independence is not a safari or a soapbox. It's a conversation. It's Who You Are. When everything connects, it's obvious. Not practiced. Just the truth.

Are you ready?

Independence
Most people think an elevator pitch is about explaining what you do. No. And it's not about being better.

It's about making everyone else irrelevant.

The BRAND INDEPENDENCE TEST™
DIAGNOSE: The Problem.
DELIVER: The Solution.
DEMONSTRATE: The Proof.

Let's build it.
DIAGNOSE: What industry problem needs to die?
(This comes from your RECKONING, what you need to say.)

DELIVER: How do you dismantle that problem?
(This comes from your CONCEPT, your new clear option.)

DEMONSTRATE: What's your proof of distinction?
(This comes from your FRAME, your track record.)

The BRAND INDEPENDENCE TEST™ Results

IT Cleaner
"Most IT departments are glorified expense reports that slow down progress. We replace them with an autonomous system that handles everything you need without people. Over 200 clients replaced their IT teams and cut IT spend by up to 70%."

Consultant Disruptor
"Most consultants deliver empty promises while retainers never end. We provide teams that work to KPIs and deliver ROI. Consultant spend for our clients is fully offset by the revenue our system generates."

Wealth Pioneer
"Financial advisors are commission farmers who structure to collect fees for the rest of your life. We build generational wealth systems that make your family independent. Our clients cut lifetime fees by up to 85% while building family empires."
Each one works in seconds.

BRAND INDEPENDENCE TEST™ Examples:

Revolut: "You're paying fees to multiple financial institutions. We put all your financial needs in one place with no hidden fees. Millions of customers save thousands by replacing their bank, broker, exchange, and travel card with Revolut."

Dyson: "Every appliance category has accepted norms. We re-engineer from first principles until physics proves it works better. We have reinvented commercially successful products across five primary industries."

Slack: Workplace communication defaulted to email for 40 years. We replaced it with organized channels. 10M+ daily users proved Channels beats workplace emails.

The Test in Practice

DIAGNOSE: What industry norm makes you sick?
DELIVER: How do you make that practice extinct?
DEMONSTRATE: What's your proof?

Write it, say it, and test it on someone who doesn't know your industry. If they don't get it, rewrite it. If it doesn't make them want to hire you and fire everyone else, it's not ready.

Your Independence works when:

Someone immediately understands the problem.
They realize you're the solution.
They question why they'd ever use anyone else.
They've forgotten about your competition.

The Verdict
This isn't networking small talk; this is your industry Independence in seconds.

When someone asks what you do, you don't describe your services. You execute. You don't hope to fit in. You show them that you see what's possible.

When prospects compare you to others, there is no comparison. There's only you.

Your Brand String Theory is complete:
Your FORCE becomes their reason to abandon everyone else.
Your FRAME becomes their reason to never look back.
Your FUNCTION becomes their reason to tell everyone.
Your CONCEPT becomes their reason to listen.
Your CONNECT becomes their reason to trust.
Your CONVERT becomes their reason to act.
Your RECKONING becomes their reason to follow.
Your RECOGNIZE becomes their reason to see what you see.
Your RELEASE becomes their reason to remember you forever.
This is your complete presence strategy.

It's your brand declaration of Independence.

RELEASE INDEPENDENCE BRAND LAW

Diagnose, deliver, and demonstrate your **Independence**.

YOUR RELEASE INDEPENDENCE FIELD TEST

1. **What industry practice makes you sick to your stomach?**
   Pinpoint the frustration or lie that made you start your business.

2. **How do you erase it from existence?**
   Define your solution that eliminates the problem completely.

3. **What's your proof?**
   Show evidence that you're winning and they're losing.

LESS IS MORE

You stopped explaining what you do and started executing. Your declaration of Independence now makes you the only choice.

BRAND STRING THEORY

CHAPTER TWENTY-TWO
BRAND STRING THEORY

YOUR BRAND STRING THEORY. YOUR CHOICE.

So here we are.

You've got the framework. You've seen what works. Now what?

You need the laws that work under any condition. When everything's on the line, rigid thinking fails.

| **Rules break under pressure. Laws strengthen.** |

Your brand is the same.
Right now, you have two choices:

Safety
Go back on safari or find your reflection like the Mirror Guy. Keep doing what everyone else does. Compete on price. Hope someone notices you. Stay comfortable. Stay forgettable. Stay frustrated.

Brand String Theory
Build something that works. Connect every piece of your brand so that it all pulls in the same direction. Stop competing on price. Start competing with your Principle. Make something worth remembering.

If your brand died tomorrow, would customers be devastated? Or would they barely notice?

Most brands are monuments to "good enough." They compete without a reason for customers to choose them over anyone else.

Your brand can be different. But only if you choose to be different.

Here's what happens when you choose Brand String Theory: You stop feeling forced to micro-manage because your team is aligned.

You stop asking, "What shall we do?" and start asking, "What will we do?"

Your team makes decisions like you would, even when you're not there. Customers don't just buy from you, they refuse to buy from anyone else. Competitors don't just lose deals to you, they start copying your approach.

You don't just build a business... you build something that outlasts you.

Warby Parker decided in a Wharton dorm room that spectacles shouldn't cost hundreds of dollars. **Dollar Shave Club** launched with one viral video. **Spanx** started with an idea that pantyhose were stupid. **Liquid Death** took water and said, "Murder your thirst." **Casper** decided from a garage that mattress shopping was broken.

None of them played it safe. None of them asked for permission.

They built something that worked.
Connected every piece.
Made their Principle non-negotiable.

Your industry is waiting.
Right now, your industry is full of safari and Mirror Guy brands doing the same old stuff, saying the same things, and competing on the same terms.

They're all waiting for someone to show them what's possible.

That someone could be you.

Remember the 3%?
The brands that are customer-obsessed. The ones outperforming everyone else with 41% faster revenue growth, 49% faster profit growth, 51% stronger customer retention.

They're connected.

You've got the framework.
You've seen what works.
Now build it.

Start with your FORCE. Everything else flows from there.

When you connect your strings. When your INTERNAL engine drives your EXTERNAL expression and your ETERNAL independence, you don't just build a brand. You build something people search for.

Something they can't replace.

Something that outlasts you.

They didn't get there by playing it safe.

Neither will you.

Make Your Brand Demand a Search Party.

BRAND STRING THEORY™

THE PROCESS

INTERNAL	♥	**FORCE** YOUR ENERGY	"Every strong FORCE changes someone's world."
	⚛	**FRAME** YOUR STRUCTURE	"Preferences are opinions. Your FRAMES are laws."
	⚙	**FUNCTION** YOUR IMPACT	"Being everywhere doesn't make you visible."
EXTERNAL	◎	**CONCEPT** YOUR PROMISE	"One sentence forces clarity to never leave the room."
	⚛	**CONNECT** YOUR PROOF	"Turn your separators into visual proof that sells before you speak."
	🌐	**CONVERT** YOUR PAYOFF	"Commitment works both ways."
ETERNAL	⚡	**RECKONING** YOUR TRUTH	"Your secret ambition is your strategy."
	△	**RECOGNIZE** YOUR VISION	"Your brand should see the same truth everywhere."
	➤	**RELEASE** YOUR INDEPENDENCE	"This isn't an elevator pitch. It's your declaration of independence."

THE BRAND LAWS

FORCE
Your **Worth** in one sentence drives everything.
Change the industry norm that competitors accept.
Build a brand they'd miss forever, if it **Disappeared.**

FRAME
Your **Belief** is your yes/no machine.
Your **Principle** makes every deliverable decision obvious.
Every memorable brand has that one thing that's **Forged**.

FUNCTION
Align your **Position** and own the space.
When your brand **Works**, people don't just buy; they belong.
Balance **Friction** to deliver the best outcomes.

CONCEPT
Your **Hook** attracts, delivers, and empowers.
Keep clarity in the room with one **Sentence** that solves and delivers.
Your message **Today** should make your old self proud.

CONNECT
Design proves your **Benefits** are real.
Trust is out there, but not everywhere.
Use **Jealousy** as competitive and strategic intelligence.

CONVERT
Commitment works both ways.
Remove the **Excuse**. Earn the Commitment.
For every Commitment, sell the change and the **Future**.

RECKONING
Stop lying for attention. Tell the **Truth**.

RECOGNIZE
Vision is what your brand automatically sees.

RELEASE
Diagnose, deliver, and demonstrate your **Independence**.

REFERENCES

1. Forrester. "2024 US Customer Experience Index." June 17, 2024. https://www.forrester.com/press-newsroom/forrester-2024-us-customer-experience-index/
2. SAP Emarsys. "32 Customer Loyalty Statistics Your Business Needs to Know in 2025." October 14, 2024. https://emarsys.com/learn/blog/customer-loyalty-statistics/
3. Capital One Shopping. "Brand Loyalty Statistics 2025." May 13, 2025. https://capitaloneshopping.com/research/brand-loyalty-statistics/
4. IBM Institute for Business Value. "Consumer Research 2022." "In Association with NFR" https://www.ibm.com/downloads/documents/us-en/10c31775c8540243
5. IBM Institute for Business Value. "2022 sustainability consumer research: Sustainability and profitability." April 2022. https://www.ibm.com/thought-leadership/institute-business-value/en-us/report/2022-sustainability-consumer-research
6. Help Scout. "107 Customer Service Statistics and Facts You Shouldn't Ignore." https://www.helpscout.com/75-customer-service-facts-quotes-statistics/ (Citing Qualtrics XM Institute data)
7. Learning Guild. "Brain Science: The Forgetting Curve—the Dirty Secret of Corporate Training." April 18, 2025. https://www.learningguild.com/articles/brain-science-the-forgetting-curvethe-dirty-secret-of-corporate-training. Wikipedia. "Forgetting curve." July 6, 2025. https://en.wikipedia.org/wiki/Forgetting_curve
8. Salesforce. "How to Drive Workforce Engagement and Customer Satisfaction." Salesforce EU Blog. 2022. https://www.salesforce.com/eu/blog/workforce-engagement-customer-satisfaction/
9. Buyapowa. "88% of Consumers Trust Word of Mouth." Buyapowa Blog. https://www.buyapowa.com/blog/88-of-consumers-trust-word-of-mouth/
10. Teradata. "How to Transform Your Customer Experience." 2023. https://www.teradata.com/resources/infographics/how-to-transform-your-customer-experience
11. Extu. "2024 B2B Marketing Statistics and Research." May 14, 2025. https://extu.com/blog/b2b-marketing-statistics/
12. 1. PwC. The Relevance Group. "The Relevance Gap." July 25, 2025. https://therelevance.group/the-relevance-gap/
12. 2. Forrester. "The State Of Global Business Buyer Trust In 2024." December 2023. https://www.forrester.com/report/the-state-of-global-business-buyer-trust-in-2024/RES180297?utm_source=chatgpt.com
12. 3. EY. "CPG brands are under pressure – relevance is key." 2024. https://www.ey.com/en_gl/insights/consumer-products/brand-relevance-era-of-endless-choice

13. Renderforest. "55 Branding Statistics for 2024 [Infographic]." 2024.
https://www.renderforest.com/blog/brand-statistics
14. GWI. "Aspirational consumers: what brands should know."
https://www.gwi.com/blog/what-to-know-about-aspirational-consumers
15. HubSpot, cited in WiserNotify. "25 New Call to Action (CTA) Statistics in 2025." December 19, 2024.
https://wisernotify.com/blog/call-to-action-stats/
16. Baymard Institute. "49 Cart Abandonment Rate Statistics 2025." 2025.
https://baymard.com/lists/cart-abandonment-rate
17. TechRound. "30-Day Trials Increase Conversions, Yet 75% Of Sellers Don't Use Them." 2024.
https://techround.co.uk/other/conversions-ecommerce-sellers-trials
18. ScienceDirect. "The strength of stance: The impact of brand activism on resistance to negative information, purchasing, and premium paying intents across different types of failures." October 2024.
https://www.sciencedirect.com/science/article/pii/S0969698924003989
19. Willis, J., & Todorov, A. "First Impressions: Making Up Your Mind After a 100-Ms Exposure to a Face." Psychological Science, 2006. Princeton University.
https://cpb-us-w2.wpmucdn.com/voices.uchicago.edu/dist/f/3051/files/2021/02/WillisTodorov_PS2006.pdf

INDEX

A
A24 Films, 207
Action Hierarchy (FUNCTION Works), 83
ADT, 108
Advocacy, 81
Airbnb, 82
Alinea, 89
Allbirds, 25, 207
Amazon, 207
Ambition Categories
(RECKONING Truth), 196
Apple, 46, 88, 153
Apple INTERNAL Case Study 96-97
Attack (CONVERT Excuse) 174

B
B2B (Business-to-Business)
- Emotions, 106, 108
- B2B Excuse, 173
BagUps, 28
Banksy, 207
Barbour, 137
Behavior Diagnostic, 80
Bellator Fighting Championships, 205
Benetton, 196
Blissy, 118
Blockbuster, 124, 186
Brand Independence Test™ 214
Brand Laws, 227
Brand String Theory™ Diagram, 6
BrewDog, 205
Bumble, 153

C
Calendly, 117, 172
Canva, 24
Casper, 223
Change Ladder
(CONVERT Future), 179
Chewy, 171
Chime, 26
Chobani, 196
Clarity, 3

Coca-Cola, 107
Committee Problem
(RECKONING Truth), 195
Commitment Isolation Test™, 162
Commitment Reality
(CONVERT Excuse), 179
CONCEPT, 103-128
- Hook, 105-111
- Sentence, 113-121
- Today, 123-129
CONNECT, 131-157
- Benefits, 133-139
- Jealousy, 141-147
- Trust, 149-157
CONVERT, 159-179
- Commitment, 161-167
- Excuse, 169-175
- Future, 177-181
Costco, 55
Creates Change in 3 Ways (FORCE Change), 25
CrossFit, 196

D
Distinction Test
(CONNECT Benefits), 138
DJ, 3, 125, 170
Dollar Shave Club, 117, 223
Duolingo, 137, 166
Duolingo Case Study, 187
Dyson, 198, 208, 216
Dyson Case Study, 182

E
Earth Breeze, 35
ETERNAL, 189-219
Evidence Board, 1, 19, 204
Evolution Problem (CONCEPT Today), 125

F
Fenty Beauty, 207
Figma, 46
FORCE, 11-39
- Worth, 13-21
- Change, 23-29
- Disappeared, 31-39
Forgetting Curve, 64

F (cont.)
FRAME, 41-68
- Belief, 43-51
- Principle, 53-59
- Forged, 61-67
FRAME Belief Test (FRAME Belief), 48
FUNCTION 69-93
- Position, 71-77
- Works, 79-85
- Friction, 87-93

G
Glossier, 198
Goldman Sachs, 207

H
Headspace, 26, 117
Hello Kitty, 154
Hims & Hers, 179
Hoka, 145
Hiut Denim, 46, 89
HubSpot, 144

I
IKEA, 89
B2B Excuse (CONVERT Excuse), 173
INTERNAL, 11-99

J
Jaguar, 126
Jealousy Reveal (CONNECT Jealousy), 152
Jealousy Types (CONNECT Jealousy), 150

K
Kicking Horse Coffee, 35, 145
Kit (ConvertKit), 179
Kodak, 124

L
Laws, Brand, 227
LEGO, 17, 107
Liquid Death, 151, 223
Loom, 171
Lush, 83

M
Mailchimp, 126
Major League Baseball, 90
MasterClass, 26, 166
Memory Hierarchy (FRAME Forged), 65
Memory is a Thief (FRAME Forged), 62
Message Evolution Success (CONCEPT Today), 126
Mirror Guy, 14, 222
Monocle, 153
Monzo, 56
Muji, 28

N
Nando's, 153
Netflix, 151,
Netflix Case Study, 186
Nightclubs, 24, 62, 152, 178
Nike, 107

O
Oatly, 25
Oura Ring, 83

P
Patagonia, 17, 117
Paul Rand, 136
Peloton, 26, 144
Position (FUNCTION Position), 71-77
Process, 226

Q
Quotes:
   Laws Not Rules, 3
   Clarity Leaves The Room, 3
   Mirror Guy/Safari, 15
   FORCE Changes Someone's World, 18
   Status Quo Guide, 24
   Advocate Reputation, 33
   Part Of Someone's Story, 36
   Belief Yes/No Machine, 44
   Competitors Copy, 54
   Memorable For Everything, 62
   Memory Competitive, 63
   One Thing Forged, 63
   Position Follows FRAME, 72
   Respect Earned, 84
   Understanding Friction, 88
   Best Performances Unnoticed, 90
   Emotion Relief, 106
   B2C Emotions, 108
   B2B Emotions, 108
   One Sentence Clarity, 114
   Paying Attention Free, 116
   Message Proud, 125
   Competitors Become You, 134
   Choose A Font, 137
   Trust Out There, 142
   Ounce Of Trust, 146
   Jealousy Intelligence, 150
   Jealousy Diagnostic, 154
   Commitment Both Ways, 164
   Outcome Over Process, 166
   People Hesitate, 170
   Don't Sell Clicks, 178
   Secret Ambition, 194
   First Impressions, 204
   Elevator Pitch, 214
   Rules Break, 222

R
RECKONING Truth, 193-201
RECOGNIZE Vision, 203-211
Red Bull, 207
Reformation, 153
RELEASE Independence, 213-219
Relevance Pressure Test (FORCE Disappeared), 36
Revolut, 215
Rick Rubin, 151
Ripple Effect (CONCEPT Sentence), 119
Rugby, Refereeing, 2, 15, 26, 57, 64, 72, 84, 90, 114, 124, 146, 172, 206

S
Safari Branding (FORCE Worth), 14
Sears, 124
Sentence Test (CONCEPT Sentence), 116
Sephora, 64
Shopify, 172
Slack, 83, 117, 172, 198, 216
Spanx, 223
SPOT Real Estate, 36, 134
Spotify, 172
Status Quo (FORCE Worth), 24
Stanley, 184, 198, 208
String Test (RECOGNIZE Vision), 207
Stripe, 26

T
Tesla, 25
Tesla Cybertruck, 56
ThredUp, 26
TikTok, 207
Today Test (CONCEPT Today), 127
TOMS, 25
Tony's Chocolonely, 17
Trader Joe's, 26, 90
TurboTax, 107
Turquoise Health, 28
Typeform, 171

U
Uber, 196
United Airlines, 135
Uniqlo, 107

V
Vision, Five Types (RECOGNIZE Vision), 207
Visual Alignment = Benefit Clarity
(CONNECT Benefits) 136

W
Walmart, 18
Warby Parker, 27, 223
Wells Fargo, 135
WeWork Case Study, 94-95
Whole Foods, 107
Won't Factor (FRAME Principle), 56

Y
Yes/No Machine (FRAME Belief), 44
YETI, 144

Z
Zappos, 34
Zoom, 26, 207

Thank You.

To my wife, Anna Claude. Your support is forever, and your architectural thinking runs through this framework. You see structure everywhere. And thank you for the beautiful drawings and challenging me to always improve my English.

To my son, Sam Every. Your direct observations cut through more than any brand consultant. I'm always proud of you.

To my family: My parents (and my mother's relentless support), my brother Jason who questioned me to the point of inspiration to write this book, his wife Monique, and to my sisters, Mary-Ann (and Glenn), and Margaret (and John).

To my friends: Robert Zessar who has been there every step of the way, Dana Teagarden who reminds me to keep going, Russel Wasserfall whose sharp editing ensured that clarity never left the room, Henry Bradford who is always prepared for what's coming next, and Mark Miles for his eternal infectious optimism.

To my extended family and friends, and especially the global rugby refereeing community across the US and South Africa, your lessons on how laws work under pressure while rules break were foundational to this book.

To Tom O'Grady. Your inspiration and work set the standard.

To the thinkers who shaped the branding world: Marty Neumeier, Al Ries, Jack Trout, Simon Sinek, Rohit Bhargava, Seth Godin, Donald Miller, April Dunford, and the broader design and branding community. Your ideas challenged all of us to think harder and more honestly.

RICHARD EVERY

From the indie nightclub scene in South Africa, to high-performance rugby fields, to branding in the United States, Richard Every has built a career on one truth: Under pressure, clarity is everything.

He founded The Station, Durban's preeminent indie club in the 1990s, where he learned to make quick decisions, lead teams, and read the room under pressure. He later co-founded the design agency Wasserfall Every, where brands, messaging, and typefaces needed to speak clearly and confidently in crowded markets.

A lifelong commitment to rugby saw Richard rise to South Africa's Top 20 Referee Panel, earning a reputation for using laws as a framework to create a consistent environment where making decisive calls in high-stakes moments is critical. Entertainment, design, and refereeing converged into a single discipline: Systems, signals, and behaviors that align action.

Brand String Theory™ is his operating system for brands, connecting what drives you internally to how you show up externally and how you execute when it counts. When everything's connected, you don't just build a business, you build something competitors can't copy.

After two decades in Chicago, Richard and his wife, architect Anna Claude, relocated to New York's Hudson River Valley, where he continues his consultancy and studio.

www.ingramcontent.com/pod-product-compliance
Lightning Source LLC
LaVergne TN
LVHW012012060526
838201LV00061B/4276